Without Trumpets

Be courageous!

Susan G. Allred

Greg Halleck

Kelly A. Foster

Without Trumpets

Continuous Educational Improvement, Journey to Sustainability

Susan G. Allred, EdS
Kelly A. Foster, EdD

ROWMAN & LITTLEFIELD
Lanham • Boulder • New York • London

Published by Rowman & Littlefield
A wholly owned subsidiary of The Rowman & Littlefield Publishing Group, Inc.
4501 Forbes Boulevard, Suite 200, Lanham, Maryland 20706
www.rowman.com

Unit A, Whitacre Mews, 26-34 Stannary Street, London SE11 4AB

British Library Cataloguing in Publication Information Available

Library of Congress Cataloging-in-Publication Data

ISBN 978-1-4758-4306-4 (cloth : alk. paper)
ISBN 978-1-4758-4307-1 (pbk. : alk. paper)
ISBN 978-1-4758-4308-8 (electronic)

™ The paper used in this publication meets the minimum requirements of American National Standard for Information Sciences—Permanence of Paper for Printed Library Materials, ANSI/NISO Z39.48-1992.

Printed in the United States of America

Table of Contents

Foreword

Within the first few days of the Kentucky General Assembly's 2010 session, the House and Senate both unanimously passed school turnaround legislation. Governor Steve Beshear held a bill signing ceremony that was attended by legislators from both sides of the aisle. At the ceremony, Governor Beshear stated that the school turnaround bill held the record for the fastest time a bill had ever been introduced and passed in the Kentucky General Assembly.

I had been hired by the Kentucky Board of Education as the commissioner of K–12 education in the summer of 2009, and I was very excited to have an early win in my first legislative session. I would love to say it was great leadership, but the reality is that I was in the right place at the right time with the right incentives to pass the legislation.

In the legislative session of 2009, the General Assembly had unanimously passed Senate Bill 1. This bill required the K–12 and higher education systems in Kentucky to set goals for improved rates of high school graduates who were academically prepared for college and for improved college success rates. The legislation required development of rigorous college- and career-ready standards, new assessment systems, and professional development for educators to implement the new standards and assessments.

The legislation also required K–12 and higher education to develop a collaborative plan to achieve improvement in the number of college-ready graduates and in college success. Since the 1990 Kentucky Education Reform Act, Kentucky had been recognized as a leader in education reform, and the Kentucky General Assembly had operated in a strong bipartisan manner to support education improvement through support of legislation. The 2009 Senate Bill 1 and the 2010 school turnaround legislation were continuing evidence of this bipartisan collaboration for education reform legislation.

On the national scene, there were significant efforts from the president, Congress, and the U.S. Department of Education to financially support school improvement efforts. With the passage of the American Recovery and Reinvestment Act (ARRA) of 2009, Congress provided support for maintaining the teaching force in each state and provided $3 billion for school turnaround efforts in the states. The Kentucky share of the $3 billion was over $50 million. However, Kentucky did not have an adequate statutory or regulatory basis to qualify for the federal funds.

During the fall of 2009 at meetings of the Kentucky Joint Committee on Education, there was growing frustration with the low performance of schools in the largest urban system in Kentucky. Also, the chair of the House education committee was frustrated with a local school system and the system's persistently low performance on state assessments.

So it was certainly being in the right place at the right time with the right incentives that helped me persuade the Kentucky General Assembly to unanimously pass the school turnaround legislation. With the promise of $53 million from ARRA and more to come from Title I school improvement grants (SIG), we had the right incentive. With legislative frustration concerning persistently low-performing schools in Kentucky and a history of bipartnership in passing education legislation, Kentucky was certainly primed to move quickly in passing school turnaround legislation.

Over the next seven years, Kentucky was once again seen as a leader in implementing school turnaround efforts and in gaining impressive results in low-performing schools. The state education agency created a school turnaround office named District 180. This agency was very successful in helping local schools and districts implement turnaround strategies and improve student outcomes. This book details those efforts and why they worked in Kentucky.

In early January 2017, I was reading my Twitter account and a headline caught my attention: "$7 Billion Investment in School Turnaround Efforts Was a Colossal Failure." Emma Brown in the *New York Times* article, Andy Smarick in his tweets, and many other pundits were energetic in their documentation that the outgoing administrative efforts for school turnaround had been the biggest waste of money in the history of federal education interventions.

The pundits cited the Institute of Education Sciences' research study on the effect of the school improvement grants. The research study concluded that the SIG money had not made a difference in comparison to similar schools with no SIG money. The study looked at test scores, graduation rates, college enrollment, and implementation of specific turnaround models and strategies.

After I overcame the shock from the articles and research study, I knew that this headline could be devastating to the educators and students in Kentucky who had worked so hard over the past seven years to improve low-performing schools. Having been a researcher and assessment director during my career, I knew that large studies like the IES study relied on averages of averages and quite often the "hidden gems" of success were not apparent. I wanted to in some way show that the investment in Kentucky had worked in many schools.

I began to lobby Susan Allred and Kelly Foster, who had both led the Kentucky District 180 efforts, to document the great work of administrators, teachers, and students in Kentucky turnaround schools. This book is the result of their efforts. It is a tribute to the many educators, students, and partners who worked tirelessly to improve the future of students in low-performing schools in Kentucky.

As I reviewed the book, I was amazed at the improvements made in the Kentucky schools. I am extremely proud of the accomplishments and efforts of Kentucky educators and students. Susan and Kelly asked me to reflect on a few lessons learned about school turnaround during my forty-five-plus year career in education. This book provides practical Kentucky examples of some of these.

Throwing money at the problem does not work. Quite often when you talk with teachers and leaders in a low-performing school, they cite lack of resources as the problem. They want more money to improve the facility, more teachers to lower class size, more tutors to support students, more curriculum resources, and more technology. What I learned is that more money helps, but it is not the sole answer.

In Kentucky, we finally realized that no two schools are exactly alike, and the root cause of low performance varies between rural schools and urban schools. A critical first step is a comprehensive needs assessment and data analysis of a school by an independent team to identify root causes of low performance and then the development of a comprehensive 30-60-90-day improvement plan closely monitored for implementation and impact on teaching and learning processes.

There are no silver bullets. A major mistake in the school improvement grant was the limitation of school turnaround models to four options: transformation, turnaround, restart, and school closure. Another mistake that is not a quick fix is the promotion of market-driven solutions by many education experts. These experts say school vouchers, charter schools, and other market-driven options will fix these low-performing schools. Other experts call for more technology and personalized learning.

These experts believe that providing personalized learning software will enable a student to move at his or her own pace and reach success. Others call for better professional development, complete turnover of staff, firing the principal, or other drastic measures. Some of these solutions work some of the time, but none work in every situation.

The only thing that works consistently over time is a rigorous implementation of continuous improvement methods detailed in this book, and even this does not work every time if the local conditions are not supportive of improvement efforts.

The level above enables the level below. Students are enabled to learn by the teacher. Teachers are enabled for success by the principal. Principals are enabled for success by the central office and superintendent. The superintendent is enabled for success by the local school board. If one or more of these levels is a barrier to success, you may see pockets of success, but you will not see a system of success.

We have all seen examples of successful, high-flying teachers in low-performing schools. We have all seen pockets of school-level success in low-performing school districts. These success stories are usually realized despite the barriers put up by leaders at the level above, and quite often the leaders responsible for these pockets of success burn out or move on to other opportunities.

Leadership matters. The adage is true: "I have never seen a bad principal in a great school." This book details the process utilized within the comprehensive needs assessment used in Kentucky to determine if the school principal had the ability to turn around a low performing school. Where we were successful in Kentucky, a common thread was a strong turnaround principal who was supported with turnaround training.

A key finding was the critical need for specialized turnaround training of principals. While our higher education principal preparation programs were very good at producing generalists, a turnaround principal skill set is very different from that of a generalist.

Context matters. I have never seen the decline of a school cause the decline of a community. It is always the reverse. A declining community always impacts a school and moves that school toward lower performance unless the school has the right leadership and belief system in place to support all students. I have found that where local mayors, city council members, and citizens collaborate with schools to not only improve the schools but also improve the community, you find successful turnarounds.

Schools always reflect the communities in which they are located. If the community citizens have lost hope due to poor economic conditions and high crime, the schools and students in the schools will reflect that lack of hope for a brighter future. To turn around schools in low-performing communities, the community must be involved and supportive in improving the community.

Belief systems matter. I strongly believe that the cause of low student achievement in many low-performing schools, whether urban or rural, can be found in this simple statement: Either educators do not know *how* to help students achieve at higher levels or the educators do not *believe* the students they serve can achieve at higher levels. The *how* can be addressed. The lack of *belief* must be addressed through educator removal.

In this book, Susan Allred and Kelly Foster have provided the experiences that Kentucky educators, policy makers, and communities had throughout the most recent school turnaround era. The Institute of Education Sciences report, which provided a critical analysis of the impact of school improvement grants and federal intervention in state turnaround efforts, focused not only on student outcomes but also on four critical elements of school turnaround:

1) implementing comprehensive instructional reform strategies,
2) developing and increasing teacher and principal effectiveness,
3) increasing learning time and creating community-oriented schools, and
4) having operational flexibility and receiving support.

Susan and Kelly provide keen insight into each of these critical elements regarding how they worked in the Kentucky experience with school turnaround. They also provide insight into what did not work in certain contexts and why it did not work. It is my hope that readers find motivation and support for their own school turnaround efforts in this book.

It is also my hope that readers will see that the turnaround efforts of many educators, students, state policy makers, and federal policy makers were not a $7 billion waste of money. On the contrary, many districts, schools, and students across the nation were positively impacted by the infusion of funds in school turnaround efforts, and many schools have been able to sustain those outcomes. There are many success stories to be told. Kentucky's is one of those stories.

Terry K. Holliday, PhD, former Kentucky commissioner of education

Preface

Every day in classrooms around the world miracles happen. A student and a teacher connect on an idea. A child finally breaks through decoding of words. Complex multistep math problems make sense for the first time. A child feels that he or she just might do this thing called learning. A spontaneous joyful hug or high five results from that moment of sheer wonder. Every day.

Much of the wonder happens without a single trumpet. No one else notices. The media is not there. It just happens. And yet there is a pervasive belief among many that public schools and schools in general can no longer be successful. Statistics, pundits, and theorists pontificate daily on failing or underperforming schools. But what about those moments without trumpets? How can a nation or world create sustainable learning systems ensuring those meaningful moments encouraging the embracing of life-long learning for every child?

When co-author Kelly Foster graduated from Eastern Kentucky University in May 1996 with a degree in English education preparing her to teach, I had already taught elementary, middle, and high school students for twenty years in Gaston County, North Carolina, been an assistant principal at a high school, principal at an elementary school, and had become the director of K–12 curriculum in Fort Mill, South Carolina. Our paths would not cross until July 2010.

In the meantime, Kelly would teach English, be a principal and a district curriculum director, and be employed by the Kentucky Department of Education in the field as a highly skilled educator (HSE). I finished my professional career as a curriculum- and instruction-focused district administrator in two more North Carolina districts and retired.

Although I stand on the shoulders of many educators and educational researchers, since 2000 my critical key learning that would impact the eventual

Kentucky work and beliefs about sustainability was around the Baldrige Criteria for Performance Excellence, building effective and efficient systems (https://www.nist.gov/baldrige/about-baldrige-excellence-framework-education).

Kelly and I are two distinct generations of educators whose lives, careers, and educational philosophies either collided or aligned as we were a part of the deployment of an initiative called District 180 (D180) in Kentucky beginning that summer of 2010. For me it was a time of retirement when I chose to see if it could be possible to take everything I had learned about a systems approach to improvement, all my educational experiences and pedagogy, and apply it to the two high schools to which I had been assigned to work for three years in Eastern Kentucky.

The offer to do this work had been made to me by Dr. Terry Holliday, who had been my mentor and colleague for nearly a quarter of a century. For Kelly, it was about the challenge of inner-city Jefferson County, Kentucky (Louisville), and this new initiative that the recently hired commissioner was launching to address the lowest performing schools.

The idea of empowered sustainability is intriguing to both of us. Sustainability in my mind is handing off to Kelly the role of associate commissioner of education in continuous school improvement in Kentucky for the next generation of implementation, monitoring, and continuous improvement. Empowerment embodies the idea that at all levels the leaders must be aligned and focused while being given the authority to make on-site decisions as data and information inform the improvement processes.

Sustainable empowerment is a model of not beginning new with the change of leadership or law but taking the model design and growing it based on the available information and data in the Commonwealth. It is agile, messy, referenced often as "a hot mess," and filled with necessary problem solving and stories of success for teachers and students.

We are writing the parts of this book to share the in-process development for sustainability of educational systems with those strategies and tools that are most promising in the Kentucky journey of D180. The work is being done by literally thousands of stakeholders from the legislature to state agencies, districts, schools, classrooms, and student desktops to our customers of higher education, the military, business, partners, vendors, parents, guardians, and communities.

The work is not being done in isolation. There are six other offices in the Kentucky Department of Education, all of which need to understand the intent of D180 for alignment of services. The Kentucky structure of schools is much the same as in every state in the United States and some form of the same systems occur throughout the world.

Empowered sustainability means not starting over and changing the language with every external upheaval, whether natural or man-made, or due to a new initiative. Empowered sustainability means learning to design key core work process systems to be agile enough to adjust and move forward instead of closing every nine months, hiring new people when data are not good enough, blaming each other, and starting over. That stop/start/blaming/ lack of continuity approach to education is outdated and ineffective. There is a proven better way.

So what can everyone learn from our Kentucky experience?

At the February 8, 2017, Kentucky Board of Education meeting, the board heard from the developers of a report on the Education Recovery/District 180 initiative. In part, "As national experts in school turnaround, we see Kentucky as a national Leader in establishing a system of continuous improvement," president and CEO of Mass Insight Dr. Susan Lusi told the board. "We talk about turnaround being dramatic, systemic, and sustained, and we believe in many ways, Kentucky has achieved this."

Is that even possible? Educators often read articles, case studies, and research reports with a skeptical eye. We criticize based on our own experiences, locations, demographics, or the funding source of the report. The thing that makes the Kentucky approach refreshing is that educators have learned about building agile key core work process systems that yield the intended outcomes based on the students and teachers currently in the system while aligning resources available based on prioritization of data and goals. Frankly, when people see the power of their decision making, ownership happens.

The systems are built with supports to make them become more effective and not negatively impacted by external factors. It is about attempting to achieve alignment from federal to state statute and regulation to agency to districts to the student desktop. It is also about aligning resources that are available at any given time with the goals of the work processes.

The Kentucky D180 story is about continuous improvement. There have been many mistakes, and yet early results are promising. Systems take time to build and to work. In Kentucky people believe taking time to continuously improve systems is desirable when it comes to basketball, bourbon, and the Derby, so why not education?

After introducing work systems and helping educational recovery teams and school personnel build such systems in Lawrence and Leslie High Schools and their districts in 2010 through 2012, I was moved to the Kentucky Department of Education to align the state work and coordinate the work of the three regions of the Commonwealth. This would be my job as I would complete the three-year commitment I had made to Dr. Holliday and Kentucky.

For fifteen months, I worked using the same quality tools we were using in the field but at the state level concerning regulations, other departments in the state agency, and teams on the ground. As issues that required outside resources arose, the same tools were used with partners who were willing to help the state department deliver on continuous improvement based on state statute in the best interest of all the children of the Commonwealth.

Kelly continued to work and learn in Jefferson County about turnaround, large urban districts, bureaucratic structures, teacher contracts, overcoming barriers, teaching adults to coach, and effective practices in classrooms in Louisville. She also completed her doctorate using "One School's Turnaround Journey Facing Reality, Determining the Big Rocks and Keeping the Eye on the Prize" as her capstone project.

By the spring of 2013 I was ready to retire and Kelly Foster applied for and was selected to be associate commissioner. And then our paths really crossed for an intensive six weeks.

Has Kentucky achieved academic success for all children? No, but given time to work, there is nothing that Kentucky cannot do (or anyone else for that matter). Improving systems with focus on student outcomes and staff support takes the politics, the egos, and the blame out and it grows. The schools and districts embracing continuous improvement are moving forward. Many of those are not just the original priority districts. Some school locations where the state intervened with District 180 have not moved quickly or well. Embracing systems and quality tools is necessary to see results. It really is that simple.

Kelly and I invite you to share the Kentucky D180 journey owned by many other educators who do their work with students believing in the children and the future of the Commonwealth daily without trumpets or fanfare. Empowered sustainability of agile systems and continuous improvement are paramount for success. Although we are writing and reflecting on this work, many education recovery staff, some district personnel, and partners contributed and are represented in the story. After all, as my great-grandmother Susan would say, "The proof is in the pudding." If leadership empowers, everyone owns the work. We believe education recovery has done and is doing that in Kentucky. Everyone can.

Susan Allred

Acknowledgments

Kelly:

My parents, Sam and Betsy Foster, who instilled in me the value of a strong work ethic and the love of the beach.

All the Kentucky educators who strive daily to meet the needs of the students across the Commonwealth.

Susan:

My parents, Reverend Doctor H. T. and Dorothy Allred, and sister, Sharon Decker, whose modeling of servant leadership, faith, life-long learning, and organizational management made my chosen profession a natural.

Dr. Terry Holliday and Dr. Edward D. Sadler Jr., who empowered me and expected me to be the best educator and problem solver of which I was capable over the past forty-five years.

My extended family of sisters and their husbands, children, children's children, and RPC members and KKI sisters who have shared their talents and provided me with a lifetime of support and examples for stories.

All the teachers, administrators, support staffs, and students with whom it was my good fortune to work for a lifetime of joy in North Carolina, South Carolina, and Kentucky.

Introduction

In general, educational practitioners and those stakeholders who care about educational issues read through a lens question of: How does that apply to me, my thinking, or my work? With that in mind this book is divided into four parts. The order of the parts go from the big picture context of education of national and state, to district and school, to the worker (administration, teachers, support, and children), and finally to lessons learned for the big picture.

PART I. A NATIONAL CONTEXT AND HOW SUSTAINABILITY CAN BE BUILT AND MEASURED: THE EMPOWERING DATA AND INFORMATION

This section is for legislators, state agency leaders, community members, and parents who want to know how education got to where it is in general, and in one state in particular. It is also for all levels of educators who are ready to take hold of where education is, what is being done about it, and are ready to move on instead of blaming the other levels and groups for not making the grade. Also in this part are the process data and information measures that are being used to look at the processes of D180 with how educators arrived at their use and what it motivates leaders to know, do, and improve upon.

PART II. THE KENTUCKY REALITY OF DESIGNING, DEPLOYING, AND MONITORING SYSTEMS

Primarily for the visionaries and school board–level people who want to see an example of how a comprehensive approach to a problem is born, part II shares how much of the scenario is a visionary leader, how much of it is political leadership, how much of it is pedagogy and theory, and how much of getting started is a planned approach. It is also for the reader who needs the human story of how the leaders operating in a vague vision get started, what that feels like, and how people translate the vision to the next level.

PART III. STRATEGIES AND TOOLS TO EMPOWER FOR SUSTAINABILITY

When educators find themselves in a difficult student performance environment or when the students seem to be out of hand, it is not unusual to hear in an exchange between educators and experts such as, "Just tell me what to do. But tell me first where what you are telling me is working in a place like this." Part III is for you!

D180, the Kentucky Department of Education, and the groups partnering with them have created a toolbox of strategies that work just about everywhere, no matter the size, composition, economic level, or levels of learning and human diversity. These are mostly organizational strategies and management how-tos. The tools are about creating improvement systems. Some of the strategies are state level and are a framework, some are for monitoring implementation, and some are for the district and school level. Not everybody uses everything all the time.

Part III shares the most successful strategies and tools based on the experiences of staff as the next level is empowered, whether that is state to districts, districts to schools, schools to instructional structures, and instructional structures to students. This section is contributed by practitioners in the work. It is also for vendors who want to see how authentic partnerships can be two-way and effective.

PART IV. CASE STUDIES AND LESSONS LEARNED WITH CONTINUED CHALLENGES

It is very easy to pass off the work of a continuous improvement initiative in a single state that is in progress of deployment as a waste of time for review. One of the main purposes of the way this book is divided is to help everyone see that there are lessons to be learned for all of us from all of us. When educators use common language and tools in structuring, everything else can be as unique and creative as anyone wants those things to be. But we must pause, stop the blame, and learn from each other to improve all systems. Celebrating each other with lessons learned in general and from messy case studies of implementation are in part IV to put light on the shade of improvement work.

The materials in the appendices are chosen to address the most frequently asked question by practitioners: "Can we see an example?" The appendices are examples of tools used by education recovery staff in working with schools and districts. There is a PDSA that is an example of a state-level process. These are not perfect examples but real examples of how people use graphic organizer tools to make collaboration happen as well as to improve communication and understanding.

If you are an educator or just someone who cares about the future of how we will learn and grow as a society, you are in this book. Find your role, find your fit, and jump in with us!

Part I

A NATIONAL CONTEXT AND HOW SUSTAINABILITY CAN BE BUILT AND MEASURED: THE EMPOWERING DATA AND INFORMATION

As a national leader on school turnaround, we have studied turnaround models from states across the country. We have seen what's working and making a difference for students in low performing schools as we work with multiple state and district partners to advance turnaround and practice. After our review of Kentucky's program, we believe that it is one of the strongest turnaround models in the nation. The commitment to continuous improvement that permeates the department and the field has created a culture of excellence that aligns with our own vision of best practices. We believe that turnaround needs to be dramatic and sustained. The Kentucky model demonstrates how a state can accomplish this and improve outcomes for students.

—Dr. Susan F. Lusi, president and CEO, State Development Network for School Turnaround Mass Insight Education Presentation to Kentucky School Board, February 8, 2017

Lowest Performing. Struggling. Persistently Lowest Achieving. Bottom 5 Percent of Performance. D or F Labeled. Underachieving. Failing. Targeted. Focus. Bottom 15 Percent of All Schools Ranking. Under 60 Percent Graduation Rate. Gaps. Specialty Zones. Specialty Districts. Priority.

Chapter 1

A Perspective on the Status of Low-Performing Schools Intervention

The titles and labels for the lowest performing public schools are endless, developed by mostly well-meaning people who want the condition to improve. Some of the titles and labels come from within the education profession itself: educational researchers in universities, regional centers, and private education–related entities have created labels. The courts from the U.S. Supreme Court to federal and state courts have created titles and labels as they have attempted to interpret what law makers intended.

From Congress to regulators within governmental agencies to state legislators and bureaucrats to local districts, many people have attempted to identify and address causes of the lowest achieving schools. Journalists with an interest in education and sometimes in selling papers or enticing viewers have also created titles and labels to report on schools not seeming to make the grade. The titling and labeling efforts have engaged thousands of people and countless pages of copy and charts to establish a name and a way to approach the lowest performing issues.

Even though they might not agree on the title or label, most readers and practitioners will agree on the issues. How the shareholder/stakeholders/customers/reporters prioritize the issues to address covers a wide spectrum. In general, poverty, parental engagement, and community issues that creep into schools and the lives of children like drugs, violence and health issues, teacher preparation, instructional methodologies, pedagogy, statutes, policies creating barriers, and unfunded mandates seem to come up most often as issues that seem insurmountable.

There is a political belief among some that public schools were not authorized in the U.S. Constitution and thus are not a federal responsibility. They contend that the Tenth Amendment to the Constitution, "The powers not delegated to the US by the Constitution, nor prohibited by it to the States, are reserved to the States respectively, or to the people," should be used to show that public schooling is a state responsibility.

Of course, the Fourteenth Amendment and *Brown v. Board of Education of Topeka, 347 US 483 (1954)* assisted public school activists in support of an American view of education. There was not official federal bureaucratic oversight of education until President Dwight Eisenhower's reorganization of his executive branch to include a Department of Health, Education, and Welfare in 1953. Education would remain with health and welfare until President Jimmy Carter's administration established a separate Department of Education in 1979, beginning operation in 1980.

Since 1980 and with a budget in 2016 of approximately $68 billion, the Department of Education has created controversy as to use of entitled funds. The department was created to ensure assistance to states. The department has provided oversight of implementation of the Elementary and Secondary Education Act from its origin in 1965 through the reauthorizations until the most recent in 2015.

The game changer for federal intervention in state schools came with overwhelming bipartisan support in 2001 and the subsequent signing by George W. Bush in 2002 of No Child Left Behind (NCLB). Simplified, this federal piece of legislation bypassed states and focused directly on schools and their capacity to close achievement gaps among poor and minority children with their more advantaged peers. It was supported because its intent was to see that every student would be competitive in the American economy.

Labels and titles for schools not making adequate yearly progress (AYP) were included in the 2002 law. From the beginning of state implementation, it was clear that many states had to change state laws to comply with the federal legislation. These state law changes would come neither fast nor easy. Getting the changes to the student desktop would also take time but requirements would begin almost immediately. What NCLB did was to shine a very public spotlight on determining the performance level of every public school in the country.

So what are some of the things educators did with low-performing students and schools up to the legislation and since?

THEY BUY A PROGRAM IN A BOX OR A NEW TEXTBOOK

Most states prior to NCLB had a process in statute or regulation for determining materials approved to be used to teach some common set of goals or teaching standards for the state. Most of these textbooks and materials adoption processes were big ticket items in a different subject discipline in five-year cycles. States would issue a Request for Proposal for vendors to submit potential textbooks or programs for adoption. From the RFPs vendors would go through a state process to be selected to appear on a state-approved list.

Once the states developed the approved list, schools and districts had processes for adoption of materials. If educators were honest, many adoptions occurred at the local level based on the free ancillary materials and eventually technology that came with the adoption or whichever was the least expensive. How states handled this process differed.

A textbook manager in school districts in one state might order state-adopted textbooks from a state warehouse. Money never really changed hands, just a figure to spend based on student enrollment. Books would be packed up and sent back when not in use each semester and new books could be ordered based on enrollment. In another state money might be allocated by the state for the books to be bought by the district directly from the publishers based on enrollment.

The issues with the processes were that training and teacher materials came only with adoption. Years two through five of the adoption could be problematic with numbers, mobility of teachers, and new teacher material availability.

When schools identified a group of students who needed something different from the text, often they sought a research-based program to address those issues. The funds for these other materials had to come from local budgets. So districts with a great deal of local financial support had opportunities to purchase and be trained on things that worked in other settings. Sometimes these efforts were coordinated throughout a district and sometimes not.

District leadership responsible for book adoptions often discovered multiple adoptions within a district, making it difficult to determine the effectiveness of the materials. When the adoption did not seem to provide necessary materials, boxed intervention programs lauded by others were and are often purchased. Those programs may not be aligned.

The truth is, virtually any well-researched and applied approach that has been developed by a university or reputable vendor can work with some students and some teachers if

- everyone has time to train and implement without fear of failure,
- the implementers talk with each other and have someone who can answer questions,
- implementation is monitored,
- materials are at least annually refurbished, and
- professional learning coaching is steady and constant throughout the life of the adoption to address the gaps in understanding and the differences in the learners.

Can a textbook or boxed program be a wise use of money? Yes. Is improvement guaranteed? Not necessarily.

THEY HIRE AN EXPERT OR CONSULTANT

There are dedicated educational researchers and practitioners as mentioned earlier who everyday create miracles with the students and teachers with whom they work. There is no shortage of approaches that have worked for individuals and groups in addressing the issues facing schools. Problematically all the issues face the schools simultaneously. If a reading program has been successful with a rural school and an inspirational teacher in Hyden, Kentucky, there is no assurance that the same approach is going to work in inner-city Louisville, and those two towns are in the same state.

As with a textbook or program, an individual certainly can inspire and help replicate what the experts and children did. There is much to be said for inspiring educators to help each other! Some of these professionals sign on for the long haul with a school or district to help the school in monitoring whatever the approach is. Others move on quickly.

All the other root cause issues do not go away. So alignment of expert or consultant work with a strategic direction is vital. Too often, the school does not know what it does not know to get started.

Can an expert or consultant be a wise use of money? Certainly. Is improvement guaranteed? Not necessarily.

THEY FIRE PEOPLE

District superintendents and school principals work at the favor of a school board. Firing someone for low-performing schools may appear to be the appropriate action, and it may, but what are the criteria and the expectations as well as the plan to make schools better? There is no assurance that a superintendent or principal who was successful in another district will also be successful when he or she moves to your district or that he or she wants to move to your district.

Can firing/hiring new leaders be a wise use of money? Yes. Is improvement guaranteed? Not necessarily.

THEY TRY TO GET MORE STATE AND LOCAL MONEY

Since the 1990s recession state school funding has waned. What was once guaranteed as new money waterfalls every five years for textbooks has dried up in many states. Schools and districts are left to their own devices to purchase materials. Teacher salaries have stalled. Frequently U.S. public school teacher pay is compared to that of Finland or celebrity teachers in South Korea. The belief is paying teachers more can show value and increase quality of those in the field.

Still, business wants to see return on investment (ROI). Should teachers be paid more and then see what the return is or should teachers be paid based on test results or some other measure? Merit-based pay has been suggested as the best solution by some or endowments like at colleges and universities. There are no easy answers.

Pensions are in trouble in many states too. There are few solutions as states are looking at abandoning the concept of pensions or retirement funds that have ensured a steady supply of teachers for several decades. This does not even start to address the brick-and-mortar needs for schools to be replaced to ensure safe and secure learning environments. How do these things apply to improving low-performing schools?

Teacher turnover, teacher capacity, and a preparation pipeline to teach the next generation are a few of the issues. At any given low-performing school there may be teachers who have graduated from multiple and different teacher preparation programs from many states. There is no guarantee that they have had special training in addressing the needs of the student population in the school where they will serve. What professional development will they need? Professional development dollars have slowly but surely waned to the point of being proposed for elimination both at the federal and state levels. Seriously? Few major corporations or health care institutions would conceive of existing without research and development and on the job training in particular if they wish to improve.

Much has been learned, particularly over the past five to ten years, with initiatives such as Learning Forward regarding professional, embedded, and coached teacher training. Most everyone who has teacher friends has heard one time or another from them that during teacher workdays they want to be in their classrooms, not in some "mindless administrator decided training." Embedded, just in time coaching can be effective. Of course, that requires competent people to provide the coaching and a commitment on the part of a district (states seldom fund this kind of position) to pay for them. Qualified instructional coaches who have had successful classroom experience can and do make a huge difference.

Some teachers do not have the capacity to address the multiplicity of issues they face in classrooms. Location of the school creates issues when there is an inability for rural districts to find qualified teachers. And what about the emotional/social/health issues addressing these very children? Whose job is that? Because the needs are endless, the cry for more dollars continues. School finance is a complex issue. Historically funding winds up in state and occasionally federal courts for resolution. Will there ever be enough money?

Can time and resources spent trying to acquire additional federal and state dollars be a wise use of resources? Yes. Is improvement guaranteed? Not necessarily.

THEY LOOK FOR NATIONAL MODELS

Example 1: Southern Regional Education Board (SREB)

In 1987 (before NCLB) the Southern Regional Education Board (SREB) and the State Vocational Education Consortium developed a program called High Schools That Work (HSTW). It is mentioned here because it seems to have weathered politics well. Today it supports 1,200 schools in thirty states with professional development. The idea behind HSTW is that there be a higher technical/academic focus in high schools. The organization continues to support professional development that has evolved with the needs of students/ schools/communities over the life of the organization.

SREB is also the primary driver behind the National Assessment of Education Progress (NAEP), which is often cited as an assessment that can be used for comparison across states. Why is it mentioned around low-performing schools? The SREB approach is a whole school approach for improvement. Often schools that aligned with SREB professional development and materials subdivided into career academies.

Can spending money on HSTW be a wise investment of time and resources? Yes. Is improvement guaranteed? Not necessarily

Example 2: Bill and Melinda Gates Foundation Small Learning Communities

For some time, the Gates Foundation has been interested in and has studied education. The foundation and its leaders have been and are investing significant funds all over the United States to support innovation and improvement. In 2000 an intensive effort was begun to establish small learning communities because the large high school, as Bill Gates told the National Governors Association in 2005, had become "obsolete." Spending a reported two billion

Gates Foundation dollars, some 2,600 small high schools were reported in forty-five states and Washington, DC.

By 2006 the Gates Foundation reported that "we have not seen dramatic improvements in the number of students who leave high school adequately prepared to enroll in and complete a two- or four-year postsecondary degree or credential." The statement was based on a 148-page report titled "The Evaluation of the Bill & Melinda Gates Foundation's High School Grants Initiative." The report was a product of the collaborative effort between the American Institutes for Research and SRI International.

Although referenced in articles as a failed promise and blown dollars, the initiative and its study contributed findings that can inform school improvement organizational work for low-performing schools. Important findings include the following:

- New schools that were opened with support from organizations that received foundation grants are characterized by dramatically greater personalization, higher expectations of students, and a more cohesive teacher community than are found in large, comprehensive high schools.
- Students in the new schools have more positive educational attitudes; they feel more supported by their teachers and they are more interested in their schoolwork than students in more conventional high schools. They also have higher attendance and, although they enter high school with lower achievement levels than other students in their districts, generally make progress relative to district averages in English/language arts.
- In their second year, new schools typically experience "growing pains," with some erosion in the strength of their school climate and signs of teacher burnout, as they continue to try to provide a wide range of services and student-centered instruction in addition to adding a new grade level.
- Existing schools planning a redesign to better reflect the attributes of high-performing schools need more than a single year for the design process. After they go through the redesign, the resulting small schools or learning communities experience positive changes in the level of personalization and sense of community, but these do not rise to the level found in new schools created from scratch.
- New schools struggle with recruiting the right kind of staff and with limitations in their funding. Schools undergoing redesign struggle with issues of changing their physical and organizational structure, defining distinctive programs for the subunits resulting from redesign, and assigning students and teachers to subunits in ways that provide both equity and motivation.
- Both new and redesigned schools need more help with issues of curriculum and instruction. Mathematics proves especially challenging for

new schools, which have few staff members in total and have difficulty recruiting qualified mathematics teachers (Evan et al. 2016, 4).

As foundation officials expected, putting the attributes of a high-performing school in place in a new school was easier than grafting the attributes into existing schools. At existing schools, entrenched cultures and sets of expectations about student achievement and behavior often became obstacles. Dramatic differences in climate between new small schools and conventional comprehensive schools were confirmed as well, with new schools enjoying clear strengths in terms of students' engagement with academics and their school communities.

Can accepting grant money and aligning local funds for sustainability for a national model be a wise investment? Yes. Is improvement guaranteed? Not necessarily

THEY CLOSE LOW-PERFORMING SCHOOLS

As a part of NCLB closing schools was a viable option if the schools were persistently low performing. CREDO at Stanford University studied school closure from the 2005–6 school year to the 2013–14 school year across twenty-six states. In their findings, they report:

- A little less than half of displaced closure students landed in better schools.
- Closures of low-performing schools were prevalent but not evenly distributed.
- In both the charter and traditional public-school sectors, low-performing schools with a larger share of black and Hispanic students were more likely to be closed than similarly performing schools with a smaller share of disadvantaged minority students.
- Low-performing schools that were eventually closed exhibited clear signs of weakness in the years leading to closure compared to other low-performing schools.
- The quality of the receiving school made a significant difference in post closure student outcomes. Closure students who attended better schools post closure tended to make greater academic gains than did their peers from not closed low-performing schools in the same sector, while those ending up in worse or equivalent school had weaker academic growth than their peers in comparable low-performing settings. (CREDO 2017)

The number of charter closures was smaller than that of traditional public school closures, however, the percentage of low-performing schools getting closed was higher in the charter sector than in the traditional public school sector.

Can closing schools save the school district money and meet the learning needs of students? Yes. Is improvement guaranteed? Not necessarily

THEY PROVIDE ALTERNATIVES

Charter, tax credit, and voucher programs have been in existence for some time. Since the 1990s, No Child Left Behind, and the American Recovery and Reinvestment Act, the American landscape for these approaches to diversification of school organizations have been promoted. The idea of school choice in which parents can be empowered to make the decision as to where their students will attend has become a political hot button in national, state, and local elections. There are success stories in low-income areas for many individual approaches. There are for-profit and not-for-profit entities pursuing the tax dollars and the challenges that such a climate enables. There are also some horror stories of financial malfeasance, difficulty in getting qualified teachers, and the constant need to seek additional funding.

The state legislations for the approaches are diverse, making it difficult to compare results. Few comparative studies exist on the effectiveness of the approaches. In 2010 the Institute of Education Sciences and Mathematica Policy Research and its partners produced a study report with the following findings:

- On average, charter middle schools that hold lotteries are neither more nor less successful than traditional public schools in improving student achievement, behavior, and school progress.
- The impact of charter middle schools on student achievement varies significantly across schools.
- In our exploratory analysis, for example, we found that study charter schools serving more low income or low achieving students had statistically significant positive effects on math test scores, while charter schools serving more advantaged students—those with higher income and prior achievement—had significant negative effects on math test scores.
- Some operational features of charter middle schools are associated with more positive (or less negative) impacts on achievement. (Gleason et al. 2010, xvii)

One of the things that is predictable and certain is that the Every Student Succeeds Act (2015) implementation by the Trump administration will focus on alternatives to traditional public schools and a diversification of funds.

Can charter schools, school vouchers, diversification of funds, and tax credits be a solution to low performance? Yes. Is improvement guaranteed? Not necessarily

THEY SEEK FEDERAL FUNDING: SCHOOL IMPROVEMENT GRANTS

Funding through competitive grants for school improvement during the Obama administration came primarily through two programs: Race to the Top and school improvement grants.

The idea behind school improvement grants according to the U.S. Department of Education website "authorized under section 1003(g) of Title I of the Elementary and Secondary Education Act of 1965, are grants to state educational agencies that are used to make competitive sub grants to local educational agencies that demonstrate the greatest need for the funds and the strongest commitment to use the funds to provide adequate resources in order to substantially raise the achievement of students in their lowest-performing schools" (U.S. Department of Education 2017).

States proposed a plan to the USDOE. If the plan was approved, the states identified the schools (based on common criteria of performance, attendance, and ranking) that could compete for the grant. The first awards were issued in 2010. In 2017 the final evaluation was issued. The key findings include:

- Schools implementing a SIG-funded intervention model used more SIG-promoted practices than other schools (23 versus 20, out of the 35 practices examined), but there was no evidence that SIG caused schools to use more practices.
- Implementing a SIG-funded model had no impact on math or reading test scores, high school graduation, or college enrollment.
- Elementary schools had similar improvements in math and reading test scores regardless of which SIG model they implemented.
- Secondary schools implementing the turnaround model had larger improvements in math test scores than those implementing the trans-formation model. In contrast, reading improvements were similar for all models. The differences in math improvements across models might be due to factors other than the model implemented, such as differences between schools that existed before they received grants. (Dragoset et al. 2017)

In general, most education publications agreed with the sentiments expressed by Sarah D. Sparks on January 19, 2017, in the *ED WEEK* blog: "Seven years and $7 billion dollars later, the federal School Improvement Grants program seems in the final analysis not to have yielded much in terms of improved student achievement."

Can seeking federal funding through a competitive model help improve performance? Yes. Is improvement guaranteed? Not necessarily

Many people have been working for a long time to address persistently low performance. From the mixed results on approaches listed earlier (and there are many others), it would be easy to draw conclusions and take the position expressed by President Donald J. Trump in signing an Executive Order on Federalism in Education on April 26, 2017: "For too long, the federal government has imposed its will on state and local governments. The result has been education that spends more and achieves far, far, far less. My administration has been working to reverse this federal power grab and give power back to families, cities, states. Give power back to localities" (Trump 2017).

The direction then is less federal oversight and school choice. Are states and communities ready for the challenge?

Most any initiative can work and does with some students. In Kentucky over the past seven years, implementing school improvement grant funds and aligning key core work processes, organizational, transformational, and sustainable improvement is occurring based on the needs identified in specific schools applying common management theory while building capacity of site-based principals and teachers.

Educators and researchers know more in this country about learning than at any time previously in history. They know more in this country about academic freedom than ever before. They have access to more performance data to the individual student level than can be imagined. They have more documented education research practices on what works with whom than in the past. So what is stopping continuous improvement?

KEY IDEAS

- There are many names and titles for low-performing schools and districts depending on who is writing or talking.
- Most who discuss low performance agree that the root cause issues are poverty, lack of parental engagement, community issues that creep into schools and the lives of children like drugs, violence and health issues, teacher preparation, racial biases, instructional methodologies, pedagogy, statutes, policies creating barriers, and unfunded mandates.

- The role of the federal government in addressing public school issues has increased from the 1950s until the passage of ESSA in 2015.
- Schools, districts, and states have tried many interventions. Most interventions could be declared failures or successes depending on various circumstances, not the least of which are leadership, implementation fidelity, and how quickly the intervention is hardwired into the system.

Chapter 2

The Empowering Information and Data

Any group of educational leaders who work directly in or with states, schools, and districts is frustrated when trying to build systems for sustainability of continuous improvement. The issues are endless, not just with student data but also with determining what measures can be used while the process is being built. How can changes in the culture be measured? Because keeping teachers in low-performing schools is essential to continuous improvement, how do leaders know that an initiative is working? If a crucial measure is teacher and administrator retention, how does one tell what makes a teacher stay or leave?

When a number is published once a year of how many teachers leave, the blame game often starts at every level as to why the teachers are leaving a state, district, or school. Such blaming is often followed by a random piece of legislation to fix the problems in all schools in a state. The fact is, there is not one single issue. Surely principal leadership has been proven to be key but is seldom the case for absolutely everybody in the organization. Thus, there must be local solutions supported by enough funding to ensure the obstacles are addressed.

What are the measures that would best indicate that an initiative is working? When interventions are put into place, how can an organization know those things are working along the way other than counting people? Unfortunately, comparing numbers to an industry outside of education proves daunting in terms of finding an organization with similar requirements for employment and types of work. Even within education there is not an official database that all schools and districts use to record the interventions being used to retain staff effectively.

Should such a database exist, how would a state, district, or school approach implementation of that same strategy? Often educational researchers focus on a single strategy to determine effectiveness for a study. There is a control population and the experimental group. When a practitioner anywhere in the country or world wishes to replicate the strategy specifically for the population it serves, those studies are helpful but seldom provide formative data for replication of implementation of the strategy.

Unfortunately for the past twenty years the only consistent measure of effectiveness has been math and reading scores with a few others thrown in nationally. The first level of that work is to ensure that the people doing the work and being served know exactly what is expected of them. Often those people must be trained to know how to work together in a defined environment clarified by values, goals, resources, and beliefs. In general, the public, whether media, politicians, taxpayers, or other stakeholders, needs something simple to make a judgment. Legislators believe that is math and reading. How can the education profession help itself do a better job of collecting data and information for sustainability after implementation of an effective strategy?

How does a state, any state, determine if an initiative being implemented statewide is working as it is being deployed to ultimately have the students achieving at the levels required for a competitive market and, beyond that, a satisfied life? Also, how do systems communicate that culture growth and is it going to those same politicians, media, taxpayers, and other stakeholders?

One of the reasons for examples from the work of D180 in Kentucky is that from the beginning of the inception of the model, D180 leadership struggled with how they could know beyond test scores that systems for organizational management efficiency were being built. And yet how could they allow individual schools and districts to address their own problems and issues and own their own successes? Beyond all of that, how could innovation be encouraged among the lowest performing districts with histories of students not being successful?

The approach was always to look for something external to Kentucky with a national reputation that would allow a comparison of the implementation of strategies with other states both alike and different from the Commonwealth. Although most of the data would be considered soft by mathematicians' standards, the information could be used to help make thoughtful adjustments as continuous improvement cycles were being built.

MASS INSIGHT

The mission of Mass Insight according to a Kentucky Board of Education presentation is "to provide leadership in closing the achievement and opportunity gaps for underserved students to drive college and career success by focusing on system transformation and student academic success" (Lusi and

Schneider 2017, 3). That mission was in a brochure that the associate commissioner for the Office of Next Generation Schools and Districts received. It was a research-based company looking for states to join its network to discuss school improvement and best practices for school turnaround.

A part of the agreement that was included in the partnership was a process in which a team would go to each state involved and evaluate school improvement processes and supports for schools and districts. One of the missing sustainability pieces that was in the original design of D180 was an evaluation system about implementation and not just results. To that point all evaluation discussed later in this book was internal through the use of quality tools just like the schools were using: PDSA and 30-60-90-day plans. An external evaluator made a great deal of sense.

In May 2016 representatives from Mass Insight went to Kentucky to interview the D180 staff at KDE, educational recovery staff, priority school teachers, principals, and superintendents. In the interview process the Mass Insight representatives focused on the supports that KDE provided to schools and districts during the school improvement process, the capacity building that occurred, and the sustainability of the improvement.

Kentucky was one of seventeen partner states in 2016 participating in this kind of state diagnostic review. The review focused on seven areas: policy, strategy, organizational structure, communications, resources, accountability, and human capital. Each of the components was rated "Needs Improvement," "Developing," or "Proficient." The two-day on-site interview process yielded a report with the findings shown in table 2.1.

In addition to the findings in table 2.1, the report listed five recommendations:

- Adapt the state's exemplary school turnaround system to new conditions (Senate Bill 1 2017)
- Continue to communicate urgency about school turnaround to stakeholders
- Establish a talent pipeline to recruit teachers with turnaround capacities
- Redouble efforts to engage parents
- Expand the hub school program

The information from Mass Insight and the report the members provided assisted D180 in telling the story of what is happening with a statewide initiative beyond the math and reading numbers. The report provided a guide for what the state office needed to prioritize and reflect on as the approach to the work and the model were reviewed. Leaders from Mass Insight made a presentation to the Kentucky Board of Education.

Is a state required to seek such an external vendor to ensure an objective analysis of the work being done? Too often educators rely on a feel good test of changing culture and beginning student success. A euphoric feeling of

Table 2.1 Mass Insight Review Findings

Key Finding	Rating	Rationale
#1 Kentucky is cultivating a policy environment and operational structure necessary for school turnaround	Developing	-Strong culture of continuous improvement -National leader -Need to maintain sense of urgency
#2 Kentucky's strategy for school turnaround is comprehensive, cohesive, and agency-wide	Proficient	-The continuous improvement model is highly valued by leaders and practitioners -Leadership is committed to building a system that supports students -Strong fidelity to 30-60-90 planning process
#3 Kentucky has empowered a unit of state government (District 180) with capacity to turn around schools	Developing	-Respective roles and responsibilities are understood within the Kentucky Department of Education (KDE) and school districts -Partnerships have helped advance the work (AdvancED and National Institute of School Leadership [NISL] are strong state partners)
#4 Overall, Kentucky provides a consistent turnaround message to stakeholders	Developing	-Agency leadership has been consistent in communicating the strategy -The hub school program is a model for demonstrating improvement
#5 Kentucky's resources of time, energy, and funds are generally deployed where they are needed and will have an impact	Developing	-Education recovery staffing model and novice reduction program are unique assistance strategies
#6 Kentucky has developed an accountability system that sets clear standards and performance targets and monitors and reports on progress	Proficient	-System described as a "balanced approach" -System is transparent and inclusive
#7 Kentucky is building its human capital capacity to drive turnaround at the district and school levels	Developing	-NISL strong partner in building leadership capacity -Teacher recruitment an issue, as is throughout the nation

(*Source of Information: PowerPoint from KBE presentation by Dr. Susan Lusi and John Schneider, February 8, 2017*) "things are going so well" can be based on a conversation or the fact there have not been many complaints. Intentionality for sustainability is essential, no matter what size state, geographic location, or dominant issues. Is the Mass Insight report a measure? Certainly, but only if it is used to improve the system.

TELL SURVEY

Returning to the subject of retaining teachers and principals, how can state, district, and school leaders know beyond that feel good test or the humorous video the teachers or principal posted that there is a level of well-being for the workers in the systems? What measures can be used? The most frequent answer to the question is that there is either a complaint process or an annual survey administered. Both of those strategies are good, but only if the data and information are fed back into the system. Is there a national external source for evaluation?

Indeed, there is. The New Teacher Center in Santa Cruz, California, conducts an online survey biennially in eighteen states and has surveyed over 1.5 million educators since 2008. The online survey provides a tool for a systematic and systemic data set for comparison, improving and benchmarking educator perceptions in eight areas:

- Community Support and Involvement
- School Leadership
- Professional Learning
- Managing Student Conduct
- Use of Time
- Instructional Practices and Supports
- Facilities and Resources
- Teacher Leadership

The survey is anonymous with educators identified only by site and years of experience.

Kentucky provides the survey tools to districts for free and encourages use of the working conditions survey results it produces to set goals for improvement. The reports are returned to the school. The participation rate in the 2017 administration of the survey was 91 percent throughout the Commonwealth. Since the survey has been administered in 2011, 2013, 2015, and 2017, it is possible to note trends in data to inform planning processes from the educator perception data.

Data returned for priority schools from the original three cohorts of identified schools and the fourth cohort recently added inform sustainability after the funds and the support people are gone! The participation rate in the 2017 survey for the sixteen schools that successfully exited priority shows eight at 100 percent, five above 85 percent, and three above 60 percent. It is not a leap to guess that at least eight of the exited schools are using the data to make improvements or educators would not continue to participate.

Table 2.2 is a series of charts showing the percentages of either agreement or strong agreement to the statements in the survey across the eight categories of the TELL survey and then a composite. The data from these KDE charts assist leadership in reflecting on entry years of schools, the interventions used or promoted on any given year, and the impact when funding was no longer available. It assists the state in determining best practice as well as where money is best spent.

The data enable leaders to put some numbers on process effectiveness as they dig deeper into the why using data questions explained in part III of this book. A study of the charts in table 2.2 shows variation in the data and comparison among schools that have exited priority status, those still in priority status, and non-D180 schools.

The Teacher Center also provides a report on their analysis of the schools remaining in the original three cohorts and the added fourth cohort. In a forty-eight-page report titled "TELL Kentucky District 180 Longitudinal Analysis," they conclude:

> This analysis of the D180 priority schools serves as a testament to the success of the program. It appears that providing additional, targeted funding and support can result in improved teaching conditions for educators and students. There is a great deal of nuance, however, and further investigation is necessary. Information regarding the specific interventions and policy changes that were implemented in the D180 Priority schools would help shine a light on what specific levers are likely to cause positive change. In addition, the general trend toward some regression after funding ends suggests that exited schools could use some additional support during the transition. (2017)

Because the survey data are available for each priority school, it is possible for schools to replicate the process used by the state to examine the data to determine how to set goals. Is a statewide educator working conditions survey a measure of sustainability for a state, district, or school? Yes, but only if it is repeated over time for trend analysis and if the results are used to change behaviors and practices.

Table 2.2 TELL Survey Percent Agree or Strongly Agree on Survey Items

		Overall Composite							
Cohort Exited	*2017*	*2015*	*2013*	*2011*	*Not Exited*	*2017*	*2015*	*2013*	*2011*
1 (Identified 2009)	83	78	75	73	1 (Identified 2009)	74	76	87	73
2 (Identified 2010)	80	80	76	59	2 (Identified 2010)	75	72	76	68
3 (Identified 2011)	76	70	63	67	3 (Identified 2011)	81	82	77	76
Non-D180 schools	85	84	81	78					

Community Support and Involvement

Cohort	2017	2015	2013	2011	Not Exited	2017	2015	2013	2011
1 (Identified 2009)	78	72	68	69	1 (Identified 2009)	64	69	79	58
2 (Identified 2010)	73	77	68	44	2 (Identified 2010)	66	61	68	55
3 (Identified 2011)	71	62	57	59	3 (Identified 2011)	78	77	72	73
Non-D180 schools	86	86	84	81					

Teacher Leadership

Cohort	2017	2015	2013	2011
1 (Identified 2009)	85	81	75	73
2 (Identified 2010)	83	79	77	58
3 (Identified 2011)	74	68	58	67
Non-D180 schools	86	86	84	81

Facilities and Resources

Cohort	2017	2015	2013	2011
1 (Identified 2009)	84	79	77	78
2 (Identified 2010)	84	84	77	70
3 (Identified 2011)	87	83	78	73
Non-D180 schools	89	87	86	84

Instructional Practices and Supports

Cohort	2017	2015	2013	2011
1 (Identified 2009)	91	88	87	82

	Overall Composite			
2 (Identified 2010)	88	89	87	67
3 (Identified 2011)	87	83	78	73
Non-D180 schools	90	88	88	82

School Leadership

Cohort	2017	2015	2013	2011
1 (Identified 2009)	89	83	77	80
2 (Identified 2010)	87	86	81	64
3 (Identified 2011)	81	74	68	72
Non-D180 schools	88	87	85	83

Professional Learning

Cohort	2017	2015	2013	2011
1 (Identified 2009)	80	80	82	80
2 (Identified 2010)	82	78	76	56
3 (Identified 2011)	77	75	65	68
Non-D180 schools	86	82	80	76

Managing Student Conduct

Cohort	2017	2015	2013	2011
1 (Identified 2009)	70	72	64	63
2 (Identified 2010)	73	76	74	57
3 (Identified 2011)	69	62	55	62
Non-D180 schools	83	85	83	81

Use of Time

Cohort	2017	2015	2013	2011
1 (Identified 2009)	77	66	70	56
2 (Identified 2010)	75	71	70	54
3 (Identified 2011)	67	55	51	56
Non-D180 schools	76	73	69	62

RELATED REPORTS FROM EXTERNAL SOURCES

Another report providing some insight into processes established through District 180 is from Sade Bonilla and Thomas Dee at Stanford. The report is called *The Effects of School Reform Under NCLB Waivers: Evidence from Focus Schools in Kentucky*. Although the study is about FOCUS schools (the 10 percent of Title I schools with the largest achievement gaps required for waivers of No Child Left Behind), the authors chose Kentucky to study because "Kentucky chose a relatively prescriptive approach to its Focus Schools that included an emphasis on school-improvement planning and teacher professional development."

These two processes are also two key components of priority support. In a footnote the authors explained that they did not study priority schools because "the number of Priority Schools is required to be equal to five-percent of the number of Title I schools in the state. We do not study these reforms in Kentucky because there are too few of such schools to support reasonable statistical power" (Bonilla and Dee 2017, 2).

Still, the narrative of the use of the comprehensive school improvement plan (CSIP) with its strengths and shortcomings assists in the evaluation of the overall process to gather data around state review of the required school plans. Are these related reports a sustainability measure? Not really, but they do support the idea of effectiveness for the CSIP, which is required of all priority schools. This kind of report informs the study phase of a PDSA on sustainability.

CREATING INTERNAL MEASURES FOR D180 PROCESSES

Table 2.3 shows the priority schools that have exited priority status in Kentucky since the systematic processes were put into place as a part of D180. These schools met exit criteria by making annual measurable objective (AMO) for three consecutive years, having a graduation rate of greater than 60 percent, and being above the bottom 5 percent of schools in combined reading and math scores.

Sixteen schools have exited from priority status since 2013 with eleven of the sixteen schools scoring proficient or higher on the most recent (2016) state assessment. Several of the schools listed received additional distinctions for high performance. The notable column in the chart for process implementation is the sustainability of performance over time after exiting priority status. Although still struggling in many cases, the established continuous improvement systems are producing improvement. In some cases, that

Table 2.3 Priority Schools Exiting Status and 2015–2016 Performance Level

Cohort	District Name	School Name	Model	Entered Priority Status	Exited Priority Status	2015–2016 Performance Data
P411P4P41P42P42	Caverna Independent	Caverna High School	Transformation	2010	2014	Needs Improvement
	Jefferson County	Fern Creek High School	Restaff	2010	2015	Proficient
	Lawrence County	Lawrence County High School	Transformation	2010	2015	Needs Improvement
	Leslie County	Leslie County High School	Transformation	2011	2013	Distinguished/Progressing School of Distinction
	Jefferson County	Valley High School	Restaff	2010	2016	Needs Improvement
P422P4P42P42P42	Carter County	East Carter High School	Transformation	2010	2014	Distinguished/Progressing School of Distinction/High Progress School
	Greenup County	Greenup High School	Transformation	2010	2015	Proficient/Progressing
	Newport Independent	Newport High School	Transformation	2010	2015	Proficient/Progressing High Progress School
	Martin County	Sheldon Clark High School	Transformation	2010	2014	Distinguished/Progressing High Performing School
	Jefferson County	Waggener High School	Restaff	2010	2015	Needs Improvement

Cohort	District Name	School Name	Model	Entered Priority Status	Exited Priority Status	2015–2016 Performance Data
P423P4P42P43P43	Fayette County	Bryan Station High School	Transformation	2011	2015	Needs Improvement
	Knox County	Knox Central High School	Transformation	2011	2015	Distinguished
	Lee County	Lee County High School	Transformation	2011	2015	Distinguished/Progressing School of Distinction
	Lincoln County	Lincoln County High School	Transformation	2011	2015	Distinguished/Progressing School of Distinction
	Perry County	Perry County Central High School	Transformation	2011	2015	Proficient
P43	Trimble County	Trimble County High School	Transformation	2011	2015	Distinguished/Progressing High Performing School

improvement is significant enough to provide feedback on specific processes discussed in part III of this book.

WHAT THE MEDIA AND OTHERS SAY

The results of Kentucky's school improvement efforts gained national attention from Mass Insight, the Kentucky relationship with the Center for School Turnaround, as well as other media coverage and is building the perception that Kentucky is a national model for school improvement/turnaround. The associate commissioner has worked with Pennsylvania, South Carolina, Indiana, and Louisiana answering questions and sharing strategies around D180.

An example of the media coverage is an article posted on the U.S. Department of Education's website, "Effective and Sustainable Turnaround in Rural Kentucky," highlighting systematic, sustainable changes at Leslie County High School through the efficient use of data, 30-60-90-day plans, and improving school culture. The article shares regarding sustainability:

> Today, responsibility for the continued progress and success of the turnaround effort rests with Leslie County's dedicated leadership and teachers. Empowered by the turnaround experts and the Kentucky Department of Education, the local leadership and teachers are the sole monitors and decision-makers in the ongoing work to ensure the improvement and success of their students. "Once trained in systems, people think differently," Allred explained. For this rural community, the road ahead is a constant challenge requiring tireless commitment. Nonetheless, the partners in this project are convinced that they are building a new foundation and creating a brighter future for their community and their students.
>
> Susan Allred, who served as Associate Commissioner at the Kentucky Department of Education from 2012-2013, and was a member of the LCHS turnaround team, confirms that the state has high hopes for the long-term success of the LCHS endeavor, adding, "They have the processes to make changes to get where they need to be. Sustainability is not the ability to keep doing the same thing; [it is] using what they have learned to continue to move forward." For their part, the Leslie County team shows no sign of slowing down. When asked if this turnaround is sustainable, Principal Gay reiterated the clear, high expectations that everyone in Leslie County has become accustomed to, and then he added, "We expect nothing less." (2014)

In another media example from a 2015 blog post on *The New Teacher Project*'s webpage, Jim Larson highlighted Kentucky's collaborative approach to school turnaround through the work of the educational recovery staff and the hub schools. A third media example is *Kentucky Teacher* (www. kentuckyteacher.org), which is produced by the Kentucky Department of Education and regularly publishes articles by teachers and staff in priority schools about implementing improvements in processes.

Each priority school can communicate what its priorities are, what the processes are to address them, and what progress is being made.

SUSTAINABILITY PLANS

One of the most difficult things for a state to do is show statewide results fast enough for politicians. Changing how people work takes perseverance and persistence. One of the things D180 does that will ultimately ensure continuous improvement in schools is a written and monitored sustainability plan. An example of an early sustainability plan is included in appendix A. Early in the implementation of these sustainability plans, data can be collected from them for priority schools to share sustainability of improvement practices over time.

The mantra of data rich and information poor is echoing in education circles. In many cases it applies. Still, sustainability data must be built into the design of systems from the very beginning, with leaders at each level securing meaningful data to be delicately and intentionally sewn into the fabric of each system for continuous improvement. Everyone in the system needs to understand the importance of the data and use the information, compare it, learn from it, and improve based on it. Sustainability measures are works in progress in 2017. Every state, district, and school needs them. The more uniform they are, the better.

KEY IDEAS

- Educators find it very difficult to measure the potential for sustainability as they are designing and deploying any given system of intervention.
- Some professional organizations related to key core work processes (teaching, learning, school improvement) provide data and/or information that can inform a developing system. Examples include Mass Insight for School Improvement, the TELL survey for teacher working conditions, and AdvancED for School Improvement.
- Annual summative results from the processes assist in knowing if the interventions are making progress toward the long-term goals for improvement of performance. Is the needle moving? And after the initial goal is met, is the organization continuing to improve?

- Media outlets recognizing and reporting specific interventions provide support and primary insight into interventions as they are occurring.
- National studies, individual dissertations, and prevailing thought writers about similar interventions to those occurring in your state, district or school can assist in encouraging collaborative discussion for comparison regarding effectiveness of implementation.
- All the analysis must be done by people who are equipped to be impartial critical problem solvers.

Part II

THE KENTUCKY REALITY OF DESIGNING, DEPLOYING, AND MONITORING SYSTEMS

And we strengthened the program that gives aggressive and effective support to struggling school districts with the use of on-site personnel, including planners called educational recovery leaders and education recovery specialists who bring expertise in math and literacy.

—Former Kentucky governor Steve Beshear on results of his years as governor of Kentucky, *People Over Politics: A Stronger Kentucky* (2017, 233)

Chapter 3

The Backstory

STATE LEGISLATION

At least since the Kentucky Reform Act of 1990 (KERA), Kentucky has had legislation requiring a systems approach to public schools. After the Supreme Court of Kentucky ruled that Kentucky schools were unconstitutional and essentially inequitable and inefficient, the General Assembly took the lead in ensuring direction is given to the Kentucky Department of Education, districts, and schools to address the systemic issues.

Since the time of the passage of KERA, focusing on how funding would occur rather than on just increasing funding, Kentucky has been considered a leader in the nation in the thinking behind equitable systems. Still, funding is a challenge for the state with steady reduction of coal as the primary foundation of local economies in the east and the concept of equitable funding established under KERA is the functioning law.

Included in KERA was a funding formula, an accountability component with supports for lowest performing schools, school-based decision-making councils (governance) including addressing hiring of staff and curriculum choices, and a technology initiative. Interestingly the visionary six goals for students continue to ring true in 2017 and beyond.

From *Kentucky's Learning Goals and Academic Expectations* on the Kentucky Department of Education website in 1990 students were to be able to

- use basic communication and mathematics skills for purposes and situations they will encounter throughout their lives;

- develop their abilities to apply core concepts and principles from mathematics, sciences, arts, humanities, social studies, practical living studies, and vocational studies to what they will encounter throughout their lives;
- develop their abilities to become self-sufficient individuals;
- develop their abilities to become responsible members of a family, work group, and community, including demonstrating effectiveness in community service;
- develop their abilities to think and solve problems in school situations and in a variety of situations they will encounter in life; and
- develop their abilities to connect and integrate experiences and new knowledge from all subject matter fields with what they have previously learned and build on past learning experiences to acquire new information through various media services.

Today in a systems approach to management these would be called the expected outcomes of the key core work processes of KERA.

Fast forward to 2009. Kentucky Senate Bill 1 (SB1) had passed the General Assembly with no dissenting votes. The bill left much of KERA intact but set about addressing the lack of alignment between K–12 and postsecondary education. Focus was to be placed on college and career readiness for all Kentucky students. Postsecondary and K–12 had to work together to get the job done through quality training. Still, equitable financing, an accountability component including support for low-performing schools, school-based decision-making councils (governance), and technology were important in SB1 2009.

At the same time as the Kentucky passage of SB1 in the state, on the national front Kentucky joined a multistate effort sponsored by the Council of Chief State School Officers (CCSSO), the National Governors Association (NGA), and the nonprofit Achieve, Inc., to develop new learning standards for mathematics and English/language arts (grammar, spelling, vocabulary, reading, and writing). The reasons behind common standards were many but the ones educators clearly understood were that students are mobile. Students should not be penalized in their education endeavors when the job market moves their parents from one state to another or they find themselves in foster care. In addition, anyone should be able to compare the quality of instruction state to state through student performance results.

Nearly two hundred Kentucky college faculty and P–12 educators participated in the effort to develop the standards. Kentucky engaged practitioners through a system of statewide networks for collaboration from the beginning in unpacking the standards, thus yielding a Kentucky version of the standards. But perhaps the most impactful event on the future of what was to become known as the common core nationally was the

Obama administration's decision to promote those common core standards by attaching funding to their adoption.

The debate nationally around common core became heated as assessments were added to the mix. Kentucky stayed a continuous improvement course established through the 2009 SB1 during the heat of the national debate. The commissioner's and Department of Education's support to schools and teachers was to consider specifically any concern that came in from the field on a specific standard and to review all standards within five years.

On March 15, 2017, Kentucky Senate Bill 1 (2017) passed the Kentucky legislature and was subsequently signed by Governor Matt Bevin, who had been elected in 2015. The bill focused on career technical education and had less alignment at the state level of district decisions regarding personnel evaluation, principal hiring, and the intervention process. Still, SB1 (2017) addressed equitable financing, an accountability component including what to do with low-performing schools, school-based decision-making councils (governance), and technology.

Some legislators declare SB1 (2017) as an end of the common core. Still, the Kentucky standards continue to go through a process of revision as they would have based on 2009 and 2017 and has been occurring since 1990. Already over four thousand comments have been garnered from the field and adjustments made to the 2009 adopted standards. Adjustments continue to be made regarding process but the point being made is whether 1990, 2009, or 2017 legislative priorities for education and essentially the six goals of KERA are still the direction for Kentucky education as far as the Kentucky legislative statutes are concerned. Adjustments must be made and yet the categories to address are the same for continuous improvement of those systems.

On a personal note (Susan): Perhaps an easier example to understand is a story I often share when working with schools and districts. I indicate that for twenty-six years I was a building-level person either as a teacher (twenty years) or administrator (six years). I also shared that at least two faculty meetings per year since 1971 when I started dealt with student tardiness to class. It seems that if we were the generation who put a man on the moon and made personal computing devices and streaming music possible, we could have solved the tardy problem if we had a continuous improvement approach instead of starting over every year.

Do students need to be in class on time in a school? If the answer is yes, then what is the answer, not just this year, but every year? Have children changed in the forty-five years since I began? Yes. Do they still need to get to class on time? Yes. So what is the plan?! Our students. Our issue. Our solution. What does the so far never-ending tardy example have to do with law? The answer should be "everything."

KEY IDEAS

- The thoughtful, selfless, and understanding role of the state legislature is critical if continuous improvement is to replace start-fail-stop-start-over approaches.
- Kentucky's 1990 KERA, 2009 SB1, and 2017 SB1 all address common elements: governance, funding, accountability, support for lowest performing schools, school councils, and technology and have added career technical education.

Chapter 4

Needs Assessment, Research, Visionary Leadership, a Plan

In August 2009, Dr. Terry Holliday became the fifth education commissioner in Kentucky. Dr. Holliday was a career educator with teaching, principal, associate superintendent, coach, and superintendent experiences in South and North Carolina for thirty-plus years. A prolific author and award winner (Superintendent of the Year in North Carolina and National Malcolm Baldrige Award Winner in Iredell-Statesville 2008 among the awards), Dr. Holliday was challenged immediately with implementing Senate Bill 1 (2009), saving money, and meeting the needs of all students of the Commonwealth.

As mentioned in the foreword to this book, by the winter of 2010 Dr. Holliday had collaborated with the Council on Postsecondary Education leadership, the governor, and legislators to pass House Bill 176 unanimously. HB176 modified SB1 (2009) to define the persistently lowest achieving schools and align options for those schools with No Child Left Behind to include an external management option (EMO), restaffing, transformation, or closure and laid the groundwork for District 180. Kentucky at the time did not have charter or voucher legislation, although nationally the issue was prevalent.

The thinking behind the external management option was that any district that wanted to employ an external management organization to run the priority school could choose that option. Three external management organizations successfully responded to the request for proposal (RFP) to the Department of Education and were approved as choices. When the four turnaround options were presented to the districts determined to have priority schools, the EMO option, which was essentially a charter school, could be chosen. If chosen, the thinking was that the state could learn from these experiences to inform charter legislation whenever it was considered.

HB176 was passed in both houses from introduction in nine days. The catalyst for the rapid and unanimous passage was the potential to receive federal funding through Race to the Top (RtT) and school improvement grant (SIG) funds. It could mean literally millions of dollars for interventions for the schools most in need while aligning all processes behind college and career readiness. Kentucky could possibly pilot some EMOs in the process. HB176 also publicly identified the initial ten priority (underperforming) schools.

There were two high schools in Eastern Kentucky, two high schools in Western Kentucky, and six schools in Jefferson County (Louisville) identified as priority schools. Critics of one-time federal funding such as SIG and RtT often consider it a bottomless pit without outcomes. When schools spend the grant funds for teaching positions or leadership positions not training to empower the next level, results are limited to that year. No question about it. People do that because for a local principal with a potential teacher ratio issue that is brought on by arbitrary state requirements (for example, the North Carolina 2017 class size reduction law) or the needs of the children, hiring a teacher this minute is the mission critical expenditure.

In times of tough decision making, system strategic planning is essential so that funding sources, no matter if they are the Gates Foundation, U.S. DOE, or another benevolent foundation, can see what the plan already is and help the school, district, or state do what they are planning to do anyway. If the receiver of the grant funding already does not know what to do and money is just coming down the pike without a clear understanding of how the money is going to get the intended outcomes, then critics, have at us!

If, however, there are programs that with tweaking, excellent action research, and some one-time funding can train or empower the next level to take on the responsibility effectively, then the moral obligation to continuously improve outweighs competing potential recipients of the dollars for the next great unproven idea.

A RESEARCH THEORY FOR THE DESIGN OF DISTRICT 180

The concept of District 180 originated with Dr. Holliday. It was based on much of his own research and the climate in the United States at the time. New Orleans had begun reorganization, Tennessee was developing a zone approach, and Holliday was sparked by a report presented at the American Enterprise Institute for Public Policy Research in March 2008. Co-sponsored by Mass Insight in Education and Research, the report was titled "Effective Turnaround at Scale: A Framework" by William Guenther. In the approach for scaling up Dr. Guenther suggested a system redesign, giving the authority to act to the local level, building the capacity of the people to do the work, group or cluster the schools for support, provide effective statewide coordination, and build community support coalitions. Dr. Holliday would use an approach based on Dr. Guenther's principles.

With the passage of Kentucky HB176 identifying the ten lowest performing schools, the design and implementation had to begin immediately with prework in the spring and summer of 2010 and full implementation in the fall of 2010. In Eastern Kentucky, Leslie County High School and Lawrence County High School would be a cluster with Eastern Kentucky University as its partner for the development of the capacity of the people. In Western Kentucky, Caverna High School and Metcalf High School would be the cluster with Western Kentucky University as its partner. In Central Kentucky, Fern Creek Traditional High, Frost Middle, Academy at Shawnee High, Valley Traditional High, Western High, and Western Middle Schools would be the cluster with the University of Louisville as its partner.

The plan design was to send each of the schools a state-trained highly skilled three-member educator team that was led by a principal coach called an education recovery leader (ERL). There would be two teacher support educators called education recovery specialists in math and in literacy (ERS). The three-person team would be highly qualified, well trained, and be on site every day for at least three years.

Through the KERA era there had been programs of state-level specialists already in place. Funding was through school improvement funds allocated by the legislature. Originally the specialists were called distinguished educators (DE), then highly skilled educators (HSE), but by 2010 the state funding was being eliminated for these positions. There was enough funding to cover the 2010–11 school year with the thirty positions necessary to get District 180 rolling. The thought was always that federal RtT or SIG funds would be available moving into the identification of additional priority schools over the next two years. Race to the Top proved to be a pipe dream in the earliest years for Kentucky.

Common to the two support programming predecessors of education recovery staff, the state had provided an intensive screening process for the highly skilled positions. Connie Lester, currently a consultant with the Southern Regional Education Board (SREB), was the Kentucky Department of Education director charged with implementation of the highly skilled educators (HSE) model. There had been several other directors in the formative stages of the model.

Connie Lester shared in conversation regarding the HSE model that she felt the most critical factor for success was the intensive screening process for participants. It ensured the best of the best were selected to do the work and then training engaged the selectees in professional development, creating a community or network for collaboration. Candidates had to be experienced and successful in their own settings and their districts had to promise to take them back in two years, thus holding their positions.

Contracts for participants were annual with the HSE though. If the selected individuals were not measuring up to expectations in performance, it was possible to send an HSE back to his or her district in one year. The intensive screening process was conducted from self-nomination in August to the spring (April) of the following year. The training for these state positions was the best research-based training available at the time as well as the best practices that the HSE staff had implemented themselves and found to be effective with Kentucky's students. Training was current and focused and equipped those who would be supporting the low-performing schools.

The nucleus of the HSEs who had benefitted from the quality of the HSE model selection and training became the first education recovery (ER) staff for 2010 and 2011. The three-person highly skilled teams (principal coach and two specialists) were given authority to act within the school to make the changes needing to be made and build the capacity of the people, every day, all day, all year.

The work that the ER staff had done as HSEs had shown varying levels of effectiveness as they frequently worked alone in a school with varying levels of leadership acceptance. Immediately in ER they noticed that by moving into a three-member team they gained traction quickly. Having an ERL to coach/mentor the leadership and two ERs to model and build capacity with teachers helped develop a schoolwide focus on school improvement.

If there can be only one major lesson that would be learned from D180, it was that having a highly skilled three-member team on site every day to provide support a) to the principal and b) to the math and language arts (and eventually other subject) teachers was and is crucial to optimum improvement.

For the statewide coordination, Dr. Holliday added the positions of education recovery directors (ERD) for each of the three geographic regions. The ERDs would be the coordinators between the universities and the schools/districts as well as within each district regarding what was happening within the school. The ERD was to provide just in time training to anyone who needed it for the explanation of the model and to monitor progress, review reports, and coordinate with the universities, the state department of education, and each other.

The three ERDs were recruited for their specialties. Dr. Rhonda Dunn had a background in Illinois as a district leader with significant focus in workforce education and development and educational administration in her own studies. She and her husband had just moved to Kentucky and would be living in the western part of the state. Co-author Allred was officially retired, having worked with Dr. Holliday off and on for nearly twenty years as a curriculum/

leadership/systems administrator. Her approach was most often a hands-on problem solving, get the job done, empower others, enthusiastic one. She made the commitment for three years to live in Richmond, Kentucky.

The third ERD was Tom Price, a Kentucky native who had worked his entire career in Kentucky both in and out of education and knew Louisville well. Price was chosen for his knowledge of Kentucky, business experience, and track record as an administrator. He would serve the central region. The three ERDs were hired just in time as training was occurring in the summer of 2010.

As fate would have it, a new commissioner almost always means staff alignment and changes at any Department of Education as the commissioner reorganizes for his or her own management approach. From the time of inception until Allred moved to the Department of Education in late 2012 to coordinate the work, the state-level coordination for D180 was in the hands of four or five people, under three associates and two division directors.

Ultimately the one support constant through the entire life at the department level was Donna Tackett, multitime retired and returned due to her passion for the work of career Kentucky educator. She had been there, done that, got the t-shirt, and was training whoever needed to know any of it. During much of the time since 2009 she had been responsible for Title I/SIG and other federal funding. An amazing problem solver, Donna Tackett would keep the financial legs under D180 from 2009 through all the personnel changes until the day of this chapter writing in 2017. There was no Race to the Top funding after all, and SIG funding would be a year-to-year guessing game with supplanting not allowed.

The university connections were made primarily through assignments by the university presidents or deans of education at the universities. Each of the ERDs dealt with the university partnerships a bit differently based on his or her own expertise, the understandings of the universities, the politics of the universities and how the work developed in the clusters of schools. Initially each of the universities was given $100,000 a year by the Department of Education to offset the costs of giving ERDs an office and some clerical assistance.

Although a very promising idea and many connections did follow with the partnerships, the university and priority school partnerships did not evolve based on the design in which eventually the universities would be providing the training for turnaround based on the needs in that region. Clearly, communication improved over time between K–12, the priority schools, and the universities, but the idea of a university as a hub of training activity as of this publication has not flourished. The Western Kentucky University/ER partnership was perhaps the most effective most quickly of the three as co-training occurred as early as the first year.

Other universities closer to the designated priority schools also have service regions often supporting the schools with programs already in place. These partnerships have helped priority schools though not in the original design. The concept does support the Mass Insight report's idea of local collaboratives. To see the ownership of local universities in their regions one need look no further than the early March tornado outbreak in 2012 when Morehead State University provided substitute teachers for classrooms of teachers in Lawrence and Martin counties who lost their homes in the tornados.

Still, the idea of universities as a hub of activity for priority support waned as the responsibilities for ERDs grew across the original three years of adding schools into the clusters. ERDs began to spend a lot of time on the road among districts. By the end of 2012 there were forty-one schools being served instead of the original ten.

KEY IDEAS

- A visionary leader must be a(n)
    - owner of ideas,
    - collaborator,
    - scholar,
    - problem solver,
    - communicator,
    - delegator,
    - designer, and
    - able to envision the system idea in his or her work.

Chapter 5

From Theory into Action

Two Stories about How Educators Work

THE SYSTEMS WORK IN THE
EAST: SUSAN ALLRED'S STORY

In July 2010, my first two weeks on the job as education recovery director (ERD) in the east were spent in training with teams from the two high schools to which I was assigned. There were ten intensive days of nonstop best practices training with the ER teams assigned to each school. I am not terribly sure what would have been better, but the SIG grant applications happened to come back to the schools that first week and we had to correct them to resubmit them. The teams from the schools and the ER teams were looking to the ERDs for guidance and direction. The only direction we had was the model.

So I listened. A lot. These educators had been publicly denounced for having the worst schools in the state. The state was sending people in and the district had written a grant. The grants had been rejected and they had to be fixed while they were at this meeting. A leadership assessment team had visited their schools and told them whether their councils, administrators, and districts had capacity to turn themselves around. One of the principals with whom I would work (J. R. Cook) had been hired the Friday before Louisville training with thirteen staff members to hire. School started the week after training. He was required to be with us. He was a first-year principal. His school was at least a four-hour drive away.

The ER team would be on the ground all day every day to implement the grant that they had not seen before this training. The ER staff members were at the training too. They were professional and yet skeptical. All they knew about the new ERD was that she was from North Carolina and knew the new commissioner. I quickly allayed their fears by sharing that although I was born in North Carolina, I learned to walk and talk in Kentucky. My family had moved to Worthville, Kentucky, in Carroll County (Northern Kentucky) in 1949 when I was six weeks old as my father began seminary. I had some Kentucky roots!

Ever the optimist and knowing I could quit, I listened to the people assembled there. They had a depressed economy. The schools were in Eastern Kentucky after all. Poverty is a problem. Coal was almost gone as the economic base. The school systems and hospitals were the largest employers in the eastern counties. Drug addiction was and is a problem. Both districts had students who would be first-generation high school graduates. Some communities did not seem to value education. Student and teacher attendance was a problem. Performance was clearly a problem. The thought of getting school improvement grant (SIG) funds was encouraging, but once the money was gone, what would they do?

The thing that made me want to be there and stay was that no one thought the task of turnaround was impossible. They were ready for whatever it was that this SIG/federal/state/new commissioner process had to offer. I was there to stay for three years and I promised them that impossible just takes a little longer.

To spark conversation and thinking, we began by asking them many questions—starting with what they wanted for their students. Was it possible for the systems they had to get them there? If so, we would monitor and adjust them as we go. If those systems were not working, we would monitor them to figure out why and then design them better together. Teachers would learn how to diagnose learning needs, unpack standards, and improve instruction. Schools would build support systems that worked. All would become responsible for all and that would soon include students. The education recovery staff knew what good instruction looked like, so maybe we would start there and with attendance.

Leslie County High School was an easy story. Their exit of priority status was the first in the state and it took two years. They had immediate results. Lawrence High School took longer to see some amazing results. They still struggle but are still continuously improving with exemplary practices in many areas. The remaining twelve schools that would be added the next year in the east would be a mixture of immediate successes, one district that would merge with another, and a few still climbing.

In that almost two years, with the dedicated work of the first two cohorts/ clusters of schools and education recovery staffs, it became much clearer what schools needed to do to build continuous improvement systems that are sustainable. It had to be done just in time, on site with support based on their own data and answers to system questions. Everybody had to learn agility as a byword.

Based on successes in the east at the end of the first fifteen months, Dr. Holliday asked me to move to Frankfort to coordinate the state work aligning the state processes to clearly define a system of support. And yes, for those who work for true visionaries, "and so much more" became part of the job.

THE SYSTEMS WORK IN JEFFERSON COUNTY: KELLY FOSTER'S STORY

In July 2010 I had already spent a year working for KDE as a HSE in low-performing schools in Central and Eastern Kentucky. Now the format of the work was changing and I would be an ERL working with two educational recovery specialists (ERS). I was skeptical of this new idea of a three-person team simply because it was new and the vision of this work really wasn't clearly communicated from KDE to the field staff. Did I mention that I was being assigned to a large urban high school in Louisville, Kentucky, that was a two-hour drive from my home? This small-town girl was headed to the big city.

I packed my car on a Sunday afternoon and headed to Louisville for a two-week turnaround training with my new ER team and my new priority school team. That evening I had the sense to schedule a dinner with the principal of Fern Creek Traditional High School and the ER team so we wouldn't be meeting each other for the first time at the training. The dinner went fine but I could easily sense that the principal wasn't sure exactly how the ER team could help him improve his school. Honestly, to hear him talk I wasn't sure if he really thought his school had any issues.

The next morning at the training each ER team and school team was assigned a common table. The department had asked each principal to attend the two-week training and to bring someone from the school with a specialty in reading and math. In some cases, the assistant principal came too. So there the six of us sat . . . now what do we do? I remember thinking that I needed to be in the school looking at the data, talking with the principal, and learning about him and his staff, not sitting here at this table for ten days!

Some of the training focused on leadership, some of the training allowed us time to get to know the school team better, but the diamond hidden in the rough was Dr. Joseph Murphy from Vanderbilt University in Nashville, Tennessee. Dr. Murphy brought the concept of 30-60-90-day planning to the table. He even gave us a template and we all know how much educators love a good template! The concept was simple: failing schools have a lot of issues. Identify three issues or "big rocks" to focus on and develop a 30-60-90-day plan that focused on the "big rocks," assign who is responsible for each task, and monitor the work. Little did I know that this session on planning would forever change the way I work in school improvement.

In the middle of all this extensive training the principals were receiving feedback that their school improvement grants (SIG) had not been approved and corrections would have to be made immediately for the grants to be reviewed again and hopefully funded. As an ERL my role was to coach and assist the principal so I jumped right in to help him revise his grant, which I had never laid eyes on before. At the same time that the ER team was trying to help revise a SIG grant, we had also been charged with developing a 30-60-90-day plan for the school. At the end of week one we could go home for the weekend and I wasn't sure I wanted to come back for week two.

Week two of turnaround training was full of more long days. We were training all day, rewriting SIG grants, and developing 30-60-90-day plans at night. During all of this I was trying to develop a cohesive ER team and start to determine what our first steps were going to be on this journey of school turnaround at Fern Creek Traditional High School. The two-week turnaround training finally came to an end and the following Monday I reported to the school. This is where it became interesting.

When I reached the school the Monday morning following the two-week training I was assigned a small office with one table for a three-person ER team to work on. It was as far away from the principal's office as possible. I felt this sent a message of lack of support, but I moved on to exploring the school and looking for teachers who were preparing for the start of school in less than three weeks. As a few days passed and I never ran into a teacher in the hallway, I started to inquire where the teachers were and why they weren't in the building. This is when I first learned about the teacher contract and the potential barriers it could cause in the school turnaround process.

The few short weeks before the school year started flew by. We (the ER team) tried to determine how to embed professional learning into the school day when the teacher contract required teachers to have so many minutes of their planning period each day and only required them to stay after school sixty minutes on Tuesday afternoons for faculty meetings. Fern Creek had chosen the restaffing turnaround model so we were also faced with over thirty new teachers to the school and seventeen first-year teachers.

The building was adult centered. Leadership meetings lasted two hours and had extremely long agendas focusing on dress code, discipline, and anything but instruction or students. Sometimes there could be twenty-five to thirty people in a leadership meeting. I found myself asking, "Who is running this building while we are all sitting around this table?" Don't get me wrong, there were some amazing leaders and educators in that building that I will forever be connected to, but they didn't have a manageable plan that truly focused on improving student learning for all.

After many long and crucial conversations, we (the ER staff and school leadership) began to truly use the 30-60-90-day planning process. We turned the Tuesday afternoon faculty meeting into PLC meetings and implemented fast breaks (embedded PD) on a weekly basis. The school leadership also had to make some tough decisions about where they wanted to go as a school. Were they willing to stay the course for students or would they alter the course based on demands from the district? By the second year of the school turnaround the ER staff had a work space right next to the Office for Teaching and Learning.

This journey was not a quick and easy one but I am so proud that Fern Creek stayed the course and exited priority status in 2015, continuing to be a proficient school. They still have a 30-60-90-day plan on the wall in their teacher room.

In August 2013 my role changed and I became the associate commissioner of the Office of Next Generation of Schools and Districts based in Frankfort. I had no idea what I was getting into but would have the best help from Vivian Bratton and Debbie Hendricks, who also helped Susan earlier stay the course. Without their knowledge and experience in state government I wouldn't have lasted a month. I was also very fortunate that Susan would continue to stay in Frankfort for six weeks and mentor me daily. I kept her on speed dial long after she left Kentucky to return to North Carolina.

Looking back on the past four years my charge around school improvement has been to ensure our processes are seamless, communicate the successes of the work, and make sure the work is sustainable even when there are changes in leadership and laws. The educational recovery staff is still using the quality tools, but we have more of an intentional focus on building not only school capacity but also district capacity.

We have grown a leadership component with LEAD-KY through our partnership with the National Institute for School Leadership (NISL). We have an intentional focus on professional learning for our focus schools and districts by connecting them to the hub schools. I've discovered that districts in state assistance and state management *must* have education recovery staff as part of that work.

KEY IDEAS

- Vision implementers must be
  - understanding of the vision,
  - listeners,
  - consensus builders,

- ○ communicators,
- ○ human servant leaders,
- ○ the best ambassadors for the vision ever,
- ○ willing to make hard decisions when required,
- ○ connectors of plans and ideas,
- ○ hands on,
- ○ willing to work,
- ○ able to take criticism,
- ○ understanding of how to work with adults, and
- ○ flexible.

Part III

STRATEGIES AND TOOLS TO EMPOWER FOR SUSTAINABILITY

We're always looking for a silver bullet. We think if we just get a little bit more money or this new program in place we can solve all of the academic problems of all of our children, but the only silver bullet I ever found was hard work; systemic, systematic approaches; done with data-driven decision making, so you have to have humility and feedback loops, and you've got to integrate what you learned throughout the K-12 system.

—Dr. Terry Holliday, twenty-fifth anniversary of the Baldrige Criteria Gala, 2013

Chapter 6

State Strategies and Support

District 180 and education recovery staff used the visionary direction of the commissioner, SB1 (2009), SIG grant guidelines, the federal NCLB waiver, and best systems practices to identify common tools to use to address the status and areas for improvement in each priority school. ER staff in individual schools had much flexibility within the content and context but the tools were common. The toolbox grew over the course of the next seven years based on need, organizational learning, systems improvement, regulation and law changes, feedback from funding sources, and pertinent data. Steady, focused continuous improvement work with constant monitoring began to produce results sparking a desire to keep getting better.

The story of education recovery and interventions for schools is a story of educators working together, using experienced skill sets, proven strategies, and quality tools to empower schools to solve their own issues and problems. The story is best told by those who do that work. On May 11, 2017, fifteen veteran education recovery staff were convened by Foster and Allred to begin to capture what tools worked best when and with whom. The gathering was an impressive group with whom it was easy to remember the beginning of this school improvement journey. Many of the people in the room helped start the work in 2010 or were principals of low-performing schools and were now sustainability leaders.

Following are the tools and strategies that worked. Each section tells what they are and why they were needed, and an example is given of how and where they worked with necessary resources. All may be replicated at a state or local level.

TECHNOLOGY PLATFORM (STATE AND LOCAL LEVEL)

What It Is and Why It Is Needed

At the state level, AdvancED had been contracted to provide a technology platform for school improvement planning across the 170-plus districts. Formerly the Southern Association of Colleges and Schools (SACS), AdvancED is a respected accreditation organization already present in Kentucky work. The collaboration with AdvancED to meet specific Kentucky needs was essential for the alignment of legislation-mandated strategic improvement planning with the reporting requirements and feedback loops of priority schools.

Although not for priority schools alone, the technology system, Adaptive System of School Improvement Support Tools™ (ASSIST), would prove essential for state/district/school feedback and improvement monitoring. In addition to statewide ASSIST, all education recovery staff members were issued laptop computers and had Kentucky.gov email addresses.

How It Was Used Effectively

Taken from an interview with Susan Greer (ERL, ERD), Julia Rawlings (ERS, ERL, ERD), Todd Tucker (ERL), and Carolyn Spangler (ERL)

"To be honest? [ASSIST] drove us crazy those first couple of years. We didn't learn how to use ASSIST regarding 30-60-90 Day Planning. So, we had done the planning with the schools and then tried to fit it all in the template. It was cumbersome at first. The state was requiring districts and then schools to have their plans in ASSIST. The good part was it was aligned with the commissioner's goals, but we were all about the detail work on the school level. It felt like extra to us."

Aligning district and school plans to state board goals and SB1 (2009) with related regulations was the idea behind the electronic platform of ASSIST. Attempting to move beyond compliance of getting it done and checked off to effectiveness was and is a journey! AdvancED became a true partner in responding every six months and sometimes in between to what we were hearing from the schools and districts needed to be different if the CSIP (Comprehensive School Improvement Plan) in ASSIST was to become an effective guidance tool.

There was also the thought that eventually each strategy would be linked to a budget code so that budget reports for each of the federal title programs could be pulled up at the state level, giving the federal government and taxpayers a true picture of how schools and districts were spending the money without asking districts and schools for special reporting.

Across the seven years (2010–2017) Kentucky and other states worked with AdvancED to help develop an electronic platform that could address the practical concerns of using an electronic platform for improvement planning and report writing. Although SB1 (2017) required less of districts for state reporting and state alignment, many districts have seen the advantage in the electronic platform in building aligned plans within districts and plan to maintain the process as of this writing. Use of the platform will still be required for districts and schools receiving direct assistance from the department.

KDE is currently piloting AdvancED's new improvement planning tools in eProve. Because this is a true partnership with AdvancED, KDE has been given the opportunity to help design the tools in the system to help support a continuous improvement model for all schools across the state.

Resources Necessary

The initial cost was $1 million each year for AdvancED ASSIST, which was a part of the budget from four of the Kentucky Department of Education offices because data and information from ASSIST would ultimately be used for support and improvements in helping schools and districts across the agency. The laptops for ER staff were already owned by the Kentucky Department of Education. Replacements were approximately $800.

DIAGNOSTIC REVIEW PROCESS (STATE-LEVEL DEVELOPED FOR LOCAL LEVEL)

What It Is and Why It Is Needed

Within the legislation, since KERA was a requirement that the lowest performing schools would have a leadership assessment to determine the status of the school and district, SB1 (2009) and subsequent regulations required that from the leadership assessment three things would be determined: 1) the capacity of the principal to continue turnaround efforts, 2) the capacity of the school council to be a decision maker in the turnaround efforts, and 3) the capacity of the district to support school turnaround.

A trained team conducted the interviews during a site visit and wrote a report with improvement priorities. The report was given to the commissioner for review and action. Finally, the associate commissioner would deliver the reports to explain the reports to schools and districts as well as what was to happen next.

How It Was Used Effectively

Contributed by Julia Rawlings (ERS, ERL, ERD)

Kentucky has been through many revisions of its statutory auditing process since the work on NCLB began in the 2009–10 school year. For the first two years, KDE used the leadership assessment process, which addressed nine standards and eighty-eight indicators of school improvement (SISI) for priority cohort 1, 2, and 3 identified schools. In this process, all indicators that received a rating of "1" were identified as deficiencies, leaving some schools and district with seventeen-plus deficiencies to address in an eighteen- to twenty-four-month time frame.

Beginning with the 2012–13 school year, KDE partnered with AdvancED to begin a new diagnostic review process, a performance-driven system, focusing on conditions and processes within a district/school that impact student performance and organizational effectiveness. The power of AdvancED's diagnostic review lies in the connections and linkages between and among the standards, student performance, and stakeholder feedback.

This process included a review of five standards and thirty-eight indicators for school improvement resulting in the identification of improvement priorities (IPs are those indicators receiving a rating of "1") and opportunities for improvement (OFIs are those indicators receiving a rating of "2"), resulting in some schools/districts receiving an extremely large number of IPIs and OFIs to address in an eighteen- to twenty-four-month time frame.

Because Kentucky state statutes require all priority schools to undergo a review process every two years while in priority status, some schools were now receiving reports from two different review processes. Moving forward in the short-term KDE continues to use the AdvancED standards for future diagnostic reviews even as those standards nationally undergo revision. Additionally, for schools and districts that were making adequate progress, KDE will continue to use an abbreviated process using only AdvancED Standard 3 on Teaching and Learning. The shortened, focused report is not intended to determine leadership capacity at the school or district levels.

Fleming

In the fall of 2011, Fleming County High School (small, rural high school) was designated as a cohort 3 PLA school. The major task following identification for the school was preparing for the impending leadership assessment and writing of the school improvement grant requiring selecting a school turnaround model.

In February 2011, a leadership assessment was conducted at Fleming County Schools along with its designated priority school (Fleming High) to determine leadership capacity at both school and district as well as the school-based decision-making (SBDM) council authority to govern the school. The leadership assessment report was delivered to the superintendent (second year in role) as well as the new high school principal (first year in role).

The results were unexpected by the school and district personnel. The results were no capacity for leadership at the school and district level as well as council authority being removed (resulting in the commissioner being designated as council authority because the district did not have the capacity to lead the turnaround initiatives at the school level). With the principal's lack of capacity, the principal was removed from that position and an interim principal was hired for the remainder of the year. Additionally, the superintendent's two-year contract was not renewed and the search for a new one began.

In July 2012, a new principal was in place and the three-person education recovery (ER) team was placed at FCHS to help implement the work outlined in the deficiencies identified in the leadership assessment report as well as the nine required components of the transformation model for school turnaround from the school improvement grant (SIG) process.

To say change was difficult was a huge understatement. The struggles began with a new, first-time principal, a new ER staff, and a district with a new superintendent with severe deficiencies of its own, amplifying the critical need for major change in both the school and district.

The team (school leadership and ER team) began working to dissect the six leadership assessment deficiencies:

* accountability,
* culture of high expectations for all,
* analyzing student achievement data,
* creating a positive culture and climate,
* collaboratively developing the school improvement plan, and
* ensuring all required policies and bylaws were in place.

The deficiencies would become the roadmap to begin creating the school's 30-60-90-day plan for school improvement as well as creating an effective, cohesive school improvement plan to guide the work. This process was new to all members of the team but they rallied together to create their plans. The work at the school and district level continued to ensure deficiencies were being satisfactorily addressed throughout the 2012–13 school year.

Because state statutes required an audit biannually, the school and district were notified that they would have an audit using an amended process in the spring of 2014. The school with limited capacity and inexperienced leadership continued its work.

The diagnostic review results were delivered approximately thirty days after the review to both the school and district. The results were severe and critical. In fact, they were so critical that the summary statement indicated that both school and district would have another diagnostic review in one year, instead of two years, as indicated in the state regulations. Regardless of the results, the work to improve student achievement continued, although at a very slow pace. Furthermore, the report resulted in the superintendent of two years resigning and a new superintendent being hired in September 2014.

In the spring of 2015, a full diagnostic review was conducted with results like those in 2012. The school and district still did not have capacity and the principal was to be removed. A new principal was hired in July 2015.

The sense of urgency and desire to move the school forward was heightened for both the new principal and sophomore superintendent. The work was much more focused on the improvement priorities and weekly monitoring meetings that occurred as a result with the superintendent and all school administration at the table. The district also had a renewed focus and the standards that were deemed not to have capacity to implement became their laser-like focus. The school and district not only embraced those "standards for quality," but they became their way of doing business daily. They also realized the work would work for AdvancED accreditation.

Fast forward to the spring of 2017. The diagnostic review results were unlike any they had before; both the school and district leadership had the capacity to support the turnaround at the school and district level. Additionally, the district became the focus of an AdvancED case study on school turnaround as well as receiving AdvancED accreditation as a district.

In the 2017–18 school year AdvancED and KDE are working to roll out AdvancED's new performance standards. The ER staff is to receive training on the standards and the diagnostic review process will be aligned. This collaboration is an example of continuous improvement among partners, all reaping mutual benefit while improving a process.

Through all the iterations of the school/district review process from the beginning, ER staff were trained to be team members to conduct the reviews at the schools or district at which they were not assigned to work. Such an approach resulted in the ER staff being well versed in the review process, the meaning and intent of the standards and indicators, as well as writing deficiencies/improvement priorities that schools would use as a guideline to move the school forward in student achievement. AdvancED was already in the state, doing work. This collaboration assisted both partners to continuously improve.

Resources Necessary

Evaluation is a labor-intensive process requiring quality training for validity. The leadership assessments in 2009 cost over $2 million. Because there were to be more of these assessments under the priority school process, cost-cutting measures were required. A collaboration with AdvancED using the ASSIST tool and the AdvancED standards, which aligned with SB1 and subsequent regulations, led to a cost savings of $1.8 million in the first year. Annually the cost is approximately $150,000 to $200,000.

ALIGNMENT OF FEDERAL/STATE LAWS AND REGULATIONS WITH REQUIREMENTS (FEDERAL LEVEL, STATE LEVEL)

What It Is and Why It Is Needed

It is not unusual for national, state, or local initiatives not to succeed because the message changes based on the people who interpret it. If the initiative or strategy has its origin in best practice or law and interpretation commonly understood by each level with corresponding aligned action plans and activities, students and teachers ultimately win. Blame goes away because everyone has the same results orientation. Conversations among leaders at all levels are essential to share the transparent message.

One of the expectations that the commissioner placed on moving Allred to the Department of Education was to align the systems that provided the support to schools and to clarify a transparent message in support of the priority work. Such work would involve alignment of KRS 703:5:225 (accountability), related SB1 regulations, divisions within the larger office, Principle 2 of the No Child Left Behind Waiver, alternative education regulations, and finances.

With a singular message, easy to navigate communication systems for ER staff, and supporting legislation, continuous improvement should have the groundwork in place for statewide scale up. Of course, with the March 15, 2017, passage of SB1 (2017) these activities are being revisited for alignment. The KERA categories are basically still the same. Work processes may change but once aligned and improved, the work should move forward.

How It Was Used Effectively

From Susan Allred (ERD, Associate Commissioner)

Many state Departments of Education reflect a bureaucratic structure. Kentucky is no exception. Often the people who work in state departments do not necessarily have an education background. Fortunately, sometimes that pays off. In the Office of Next Generation Schools and Districts in the Kentucky Department of Education were (already mentioned in Kelly's story) Vivian Bratton, the administrative professional, and Debbie Hendricks, the policy advisor for the two offices that Allred was charged with merging. Both could have retired many years ago and thankfully had not.

Vivian made sure the novice to bureaucracy associate commissioner understood how things worked in a bureaucracy no matter how outrageous they seemed. Hendricks did not flinch when asked to research all the Kentucky statutes that impacted the two offices. With eternal smiles and incredible work ethic the two guided the work through what already existed and helped develop the draft of the regulation that would keep the work moving forward. It was the role of the associate commissioner to be sure the people doing the work understood why the work was needed. Hendricks and Bratton caught on fast!

The 703KAR5:225 document was used to provide the backbone for the work focused on continuous improvement while still respecting all the statutes that were in place. Kentucky, like most states, did not need new laws. The laws on the books needed to be enforced and clarified. Workers needed to be sure processes in the department were aligned. Of course, there was about a minute to do that! Throughout the time together the unofficial mantra in the office was "Why are we doing this, how does it help us help children, and where is it in writing?"

Resources Necessary

Having leaders at each level who have common understanding of the vision, common documents, and common language is essential. To achieve that level of collaborative leadership among all stakeholders is a challenge. Constant reinforcement from the commissioner and the State Board of Education was helpful. Education recovery training started out rocky but has become aligned and improves based on regional performance.

For example, in the summer of 2016, Jefferson County priority school teachers and educational recovery staff started designing and delivering "priority school training" to incoming priority school teachers. This type of collaboration and intentional training was unheard of in 2010. Time and professional learning resources, common documents, and streamlined communication are key resource necessary components as well as leadership at the state level.

30-60-90-DAY PLANNING (LOCAL LEVEL) (APPENDIX B)

What It Is and Why It Is Needed

One of the takeaways from the infamous two weeks of training in Louisville (July 2010) when teams met with ER staff for the first time was the idea of a very agile, flexible, well-monitored, and changeable planning process every thirty days as mentioned by Kelly in her story. Dr. Joe Murphy spent a day with those assembled for priority training in Louisville to discuss the concept of 30-60-90-day planning. It only made sense, after all, to change the things that are not working with students as the strategies are identified through monitoring of student progress. The foundation of the plan was to identify three big rocks, or three key strategic issues, that if they were addressed would result in the most improvement. Each school would identify the big rocks based on its own data (aligned with school improvement grant goals) and start to work.

The tool was embraced by the ERDs because it would be a way to have written evidence of systems being built to yield intended results and get us all started. But could it be every thirty days?

How It Was Used Effectively

Contributed by Susan Greer-Leslie (ERL, ERD) (Rural example, tool used at all levels)

As ER directors/staff members approach a newly identified low-performing school, we deal with turnaround principles or criteria within change models. A key premise is the school's improvement plan. When typical school leaders (priority or not) are asked about the location of their school improvement plan that guides the work, many times an awkward pause ensues. The answer is sometimes vague or simply "on the state platform." This fact led many to realize a real, living plan must exist governing the work in manageable chunks to be monitored and assessed for continual next steps.

The seed for 30-60-90-day planning was planted by Dr. Murphy during the first two-week marathon turnaround training. Our goal for the two-week period was to analyze our school data and to prioritize "three big rocks" or priorities for improvement that if handled would leverage and address many other issues. Upon selection of these, we would also need thirty days of actionable steps for each big rock.

With the beginning of this work, as the ERL assigned to Leslie County, we had functioned more as a work group and not necessarily as an effective team.

Our leadership team had worked collaboratively on several important items but not necessarily sharing the completion of work around an identified priority with the actionable steps being amended for effectiveness. The team and the plan were kind of the chicken or the egg scenario. Our team promulgated the plan and the need to carry out the plan for systematic work promulgated the need for an effective team.

In year one of the school improvement grant process, we began building an effective leadership team and created the big rocks and the first thirty days of actionable steps together. We then created sixty days and skipped to the 180-day plan to work backward with the end in mind to fill in the activities between.

Our meetings were structured and included progress monitoring of the plan each time. As a team, we color coded the progress of each activity: green highlighting signaled the completion of an activity and yellow highlighting signaled the activity had begun but was not completed or needed to be rethought.

One of the first issues we faced as our team developed the plan was planning an excessive number of activities for each thirty-day period. During the first thirty days, we attempted to not only reach our yearly goal in thirty days but also to cure world hunger in the process! Over time, we became much more realistic with how many actionable steps were doable in chunks toward the goals. Beyond the leadership team meetings, the plan continued to drive the work as it was deployed then to PLC leaders through their weekly meeting and then to teachers during the PLC meetings.

One other conflict we faced was the timing of the ER staff turning the plan over to the school leadership. We turned it over eventually but continued to take it back any time there was a concern. The created meeting structure kept the plan alive and guiding daily work and behaviors.

Another beauty of the 30-60-90-day plan was that color coding the activities exposed existing barriers and issues when it became impossible to implement the activities without performing other work. Student attendance was an issue that impacted numerous activities and was a barrier to goal achievement. As attendance continued to surface, it became obvious that we would have to use a quality tool, PDSA, to address this. The person responsible for an issue formed a study team to lead the development of the PDSA, which was then monitored by the leadership team.

The team and the plan kept our team grounded in systematic, continuous improvement work. Upon discussion with these team members recently, the unanimous feeling was that once you have been part of a high-functioning team whose steps are directed by a real, timely plan, you are constantly searching to replicate this experience!

Resources Necessary

30-60-90-day planning was done with a template provided by Dr. Murphy, having been adjusted over time for education recovery. The template was free. As ER staff in the schools began to use it and improve it, some common training was developed for its use. Time to plan and monitor is the greatest resource requirement. Having the three-member ER team on site every day makes the monitoring more manageable. Slowly but surely the plan becomes the way the schools work.

THE ART OF SYSTEM QUESTIONING/DATA QUESTIONS (STATE AND LOCAL) (APPENDIX C)

What It Is and Why It Is Needed

Using questions about systems rather than suggesting answers and solutions is not a new management approach. Frequently in school situations, however, problems are identified, a money source located, and then a search for a product or expert to address the situation is pursued. When the product or expert is engaged, training occurs and then the product or expert's advice is implemented with varying degrees of success based on the design for deployment and monitoring.

Knowing that funding was limited and the direction for scale up had to be through building of capacity of the schools and districts, an examination of systems to deliver the desired results became the Kentucky approach. The 30-60-90-day plans were the vehicle. The methodology would be questioning.

Across seven years, the Baldrige performance excellence categories for systems began to be used as a basis for looking at systems in education recovery work in Kentucky. At the beginning, the questioning that was used in common was based on the work of Dr. Edie Holcomb, who taught at Wichita State and was noted for her ability to link research to practice.

To analyze data, she suggested asking five questions and we added a sixth.

1) What questions are we trying to answer with the information/data?
2) What does the data/information tell us?
3) What does the data/information not tell us?
4) What are causes for celebration?
5) What are the opportunities for improvement? And we added,
6) What do we do next?

The data questions or data-wise questions, as they are referenced in Kentucky, are used in many kinds of settings including the ASSIST platform for school improvement plans, the diagnostic review process, and the beginning work in coaching teachers as to how to examine and use data to improve student performance. They are essential in the 30-60-90-day planning process for determining what happens next.

Other systems questions regarding the nature of how systems are designed began to be used as appropriate, but level one was the Kentucky data questions.

How It Was Used Effectively

Contributed by Todd Tucker (ERL) (rural example, tool used at all levels)

Implementing the systems approach to school improvement, the leadership team leveraged data shared in PLCs on common assessments to create the need for improvement. The approach at Pulaski County High School was totally different than the approach at Caverna High School where I first served as an ERL. Previously, I saw my role as analyzing data from the school's report card and the diagnostic review to determine where we needed to focus our time, efforts, and resources. This approach had limited success.

The systems questioning approach enabled the leadership to engage the stakeholders at the school to own their path to school improvement. Using the PLC as the vehicle for analyzing data enabled the leadership to create a need for improvement. The data collected and analyzed by teachers using data questions on common summative assessment along with student perception data on plus/deltas became our leverage for school improvement. No longer were we suggesting what the stakeholders needed to do to improve.

Through focused, intentional questioning and modeling how to analyze the data we helped teachers uncover those gaps and then provided support in reducing or eliminating those gaps. Teachers became owners of the need to improve. This allowed us to create a culture of continuous improvement. Teachers were provided a systematic process to improve and administrators to monitor teachers' curriculum, instruction, and assessment practices through using data questions.

Resources Necessary

Data questions are one of the ER District 180 mainstays because they can be used spontaneously for no money! There are few places in Kentucky education one can go where people do not know them. It is the backbone of how the PLCs work. The resources are time and leaders who will use them.

PROFESSIONAL LEARNING COMMUNITIES (PLCS) (LOCAL LEVEL) (APPENDIX D)

What It Is and Why It Is Needed

Dr. Richard and Rebecca DuFour's work regarding the professional learning communities has proven important in creating effective working teams. The book *Learning by Doing* had been given to all Kentucky schools prior to 2010 with regional trainings accompanied by many visits to Kentucky by the DuFours. Because that training had already occurred and there was the need for a consistent model for communication in schools, the PLC was to be the vehicle for in-school teacher collaboration. Having consistency about how communication would occur within the schools was essential to ensuring the improvement message was the same at every level.

How It Was Used Effectively Part I

Contributed by Kelly Foster (ERL Fern Creek, Associate Commissioner) (large, urban high school)

In 2010 Fern Creek High School was adult-centered, it lacked a schoolwide curriculum, teachers were unclear about standards, and the instruction was far from rigorous. They desperately needed to implement professional learning communities (PLCs), but the challenge was selling this to the staff and figuring out how to develop a PLC process around the teacher contract.

PLCs in the first year were far from exemplar, but the school leadership was willing to give up the weekly faculty meeting and teachers were meeting together each week in content teams. This was a start! The DuFour work was the guide that was used to build their PLC process.

By year two of the turnaround process we had teacher leaders running the PLC meetings and creating agendas. School leadership began to see the value of this work and helped ensure a process was developed in which student data was being used in PLC meetings to make true instructional decisions to improve student learning.

The PLC structure is the backbone of Fern Creek. Plain and simple. It is how they operate and how they continue to improve. In 2016, they presented their "change story" as the winner of the $10,000 School Improvement and Change award given by the National Principal Leadership Institute in New York. In 2017, they received the DuFour Award, a $25,000 award named in honor of Rick DuFour that recognizes one outstanding PLC demonstrating exceptional levels of student achievement.

How It Was Used Effectively Part II

Contributed by Todd Tucker (Pulaski) (rural high school)

The PLC protocol provided a structure for all teachers to participate in collaborative learning communities meeting both informally and formally on a regular schedule to inform the ongoing modification of instruction and provide data for possible curriculum revision. The process also provided students with specific and immediate feedback about their learning.

The leadership team used the common planning periods to develop a foundation to understanding the essential elements of PLCs. The PLC structure enabled teachers to connect and align the systems approach currently employed in their classroom along with the multiple measures of Kentucky's Teacher Performance Growth and Effectiveness System (TPGES) by engaging their colleagues in conversations surrounding the data and taking ownership of the PDSA continuous improvement cycle to improve student achievement. Aligning the PLC protocol to TPGES promotes the vision of continuous professional growth and development of skills needed to be a highly effective teacher.

Within the *Plan, Do, Study, Act* cycle, teachers were doing a good job with the *planning* and *doing* but often fell short in *studying* the results of strategies used for the learning cycle and improving (*acting*) based on the data. Pulaski County High School was a school with no shortage of teachers working hard. The PLC protocol created an organizational structure that aligned our school improvement efforts with the vision of the Kentucky Department of Education. The PLC protocol moved our efforts for improvement to the classroom and student level. This blueprint for continuous and sustainable improvement allowed us to capitalize on a collective effort to move toward shared purpose, values, and goals.

The PLC protocol design allowed administrators to monitor the school's curriculum, instructional design, and assessment practices to ensure teacher effectiveness and most importantly student learning. Using data from three-week common assessments and an examination of professional practice, teachers and administrators systematically monitored and adjusted curriculum, instruction, and assessment to ensure alignment with the school's delivery targets and vision of graduating all students to be college and/or career ready.

Resources Necessary

Perhaps the greatest resource for effective PLCs is leadership commitment to making them work, a defined systematic process that everyone understands, and time to determine how it best suits the working environment.

USE OF PLAN(P) DO(D) STUDY(S) ACT(A) AS AN IMPROVEMENT PROCESS (STATE AND LOCAL LEVEL) (APPENDIX E)

What It Is and Why It Is Needed

Having a common improvement planning template ensures that whatever the process or system that needs to be improved is, the process followed would be the same. The PDSA or PDC(check)A has been used in quality management work at least since the 1980s. The elements of it are the same needed in implementing W. Edwards Deming's ideas behind his quotes: "If you can't describe what you are doing as a process, you don't know what you are doing" and "94% of problems in organizations are systems driven and only 6% are people driven."

Having a common approach to addressing a problem makes it easier to transfer knowledge from one school or district to another and inform the overall work. PDSAs are now used regularly in Department of Education work as evidenced in the novice reduction initiative and state management and assistance work for state intervention.

How It Was Used Effectively

Taken from an interview with Jim Hamm (ERL, State Manager) (district in financial crisis had to merge with another district)

Jim Hamm began as an education recovery leader at Monticello High School in Eastern Kentucky. Not many weeks into his assignment it was evident that the small district was in serious financial trouble. As Jim began to explore what was happening in the district, he shared the information with Associate Commissioner Allred and then-associate Hiren Desai in finance. The conversations became more focused on another Kentucky statute regarding state assistance or management, opening conversations with the Kentucky Board of Education. Jim was clearly the man for the moment.

Hamm continued to lead the high school ER team as he negotiated what the district needed to do. Within a year, Jim led the schools and district using PDSA processes to merge with another school district. For those reading this work who have had to address similar issues, a year for a merger is remarkable. We found in Jim Hamm an absolute asset for groundwork in assistance and management processes from then until his recent retirement.

Jim Hamm attributes improvement at the district, school, and classroom levels to the use of the PDSA. He indicated that he was finding that most districts or schools in trouble have good people but they are working in bad systems. So to him the work was to build good system processes that produce successful results. Repeating the processes and improving the processes are then owned by the people who helped create them. People learn to work smarter, not harder. The more the systems' processes are used, the easier it gets to address issues and solve problems.

Often Jim found that from the PDSA would grow action steps for 30-60-90-day planning that became the way of the work for everyone. By monitoring the PDSA/plan validation for the work, processes focused on goals became easier and easier.

Jim's words: "One thing that sticks out to me about PDSAs is that the tool validates the work done by the districts. It gives them a sense of accomplishment. Nothing is worse than getting used to losing. It is almost like people working in a bad system are working so hard and getting the same results repeatedly. The PDSA process breaks that cycle of expecting to lose by taking away excuses and by validating people's work. It memorializes the work. Success is contagious in that kind of environment. PDSAs show how all the little steps in the process must be written out and put to a specific timeline. Most people in broken systems have good intentions but never seem to get the important work done (big rocks) because of all the constant distractions caused by working in those systems. There are always more distractions because there are no specific processes and procedures to fix problems. Those problems then become bigger problems. It is exponential."

Although this book is not about state management and assistance, the tools being used are similar for improvement. The issues are real. For example, J. D. Vance in his autobiographical *Hillbilly Elegy* referenced the first management district, Breathitt, saying, "The public schools are so bad that the state of Kentucky recently seized control" (Vance 2016, 19).

Taking over a district like Breathitt meant a rocky start but they now have functional PDSAs that are driving the improvement priorities. A significant difference is happening in student achievement and in the perception of the community about the schools as evidenced by a June 2017 vote by the Board of Education and subsequent September vote by the community to raise the allowable tax rate to the maximum "5 cents," which would have been unheard of in 2012 when management began.

In two other management districts, Robertson and Fleming, Jim Hamm started by working with staff on PDSAs for every aspect of the organization: governance, food service, transportation, curriculum, and instruction and helping them realize that they had a way out of management (recently granted in June 2017) and fiscal sustainability.

As is often said in educational recovery work, the culture changes positively when the message is clear, everybody understands the message, and the message does not change based on the politics of the organization. ER staff has also played roles in these schools.

Resources Necessary

One of the reasons the PDSA is considered one of the basic tools is that it is free! Leadership must be committed to using the tool for design and analysis of the issue/system, the action plan, and then monitoring of it. PDSA must be modeled by leaders. It is crucial for continuous improvement as its monitoring creates new action for improvement.

SPECIAL TWO-WAY PARTNERSHIPS

What It Is and Why It Is Needed

When there are few or no new dollars to assist in implementing an initiative, state departments need to look at existing partnerships to determine how they are working. They need to see if adjusting and working together can ensure that support systems are aligned with the focus and goals of the initiative. If the reader were to ask most Kentucky districts to describe 2009–11, they would say that there was so much new. There was new accountability, new standards, new teacher evaluation, new technology platforms, and new NCLB language.

So how can the message be simplified enough that everyone is moving in the same direction? College and career readiness became a target for focus. For District 180 there were specific needs to ensure that schools were focused on college and career readiness for all students and that they had systems to get them there. It was that common language of closing gaps for college and career readiness that began to be used in working with all partners/vendors. Particularly helpful and willing to adjust their processes to meet our needs were the following.

AdvancED. The former Southern Association of Colleges and Schools (SACS) has been an accrediting agency for many years. Over seven hundred schools in Kentucky were already using AdvancED as an accrediting body. What if KDE aligned the school improvement planning process with the AdvancED standards of stable governance, coherent course of study, a reliable system by which to assess students' progress, instructors who have a clear understanding of what they aim to teach, how, and why, and access to the resources they need? KDE checked to see if aligning the leadership assessment process with these same standards also aligned with SB1 (2009) and regulations. Then KDE asked AdvancED to help design that diagnostic review process.

As mentioned previously KDE costs the first year of the change went from a little over $2 million to $200,000 for the review process. The collaboration with AdvancED continues to be mutually helpful. Jerry Cooper, current vice president, Central Region USA, indicated he believes what started the collaboration was a mutual respect for common goals and a willingness to work together to fix the things that were not helping KDE help schools and districts. As the partnership has evolved, KDE and AdvancED have become mutual problem solvers. The work that Kentucky does with ER staff training has informed the work that AdvancED does in other states. PDSAs were created for these collaborations.

Council of Chief State School Officers. The Council of Chief State School Officers (CCSSO) has been a consistent partner throughout this journey. Current associate commissioner Foster has been asked several times to present Kentucky's work during CCSSO webinars and calls. CCSSO has helped states come together to discuss best practices and SIG implementation. CCSSO has coordinated opportunities for states to discuss the implementation of ESSA and provided guidance around developing state plans under ESSA.

Center for School Turnaround. The Center for School Turnaround has been a resource that enables states to come together at conferences and conference calls to hear how other states are handling the challenges of school improvement. Dr. Foster was asked to serve on their leadership council in 2015 and participates on bimonthly calls with state leaders. She has been asked to share Kentucky's school improvement work on numerous calls. This interaction has led to having one-on-one discussions with Louisiana, Indiana, Pennsylvania, South Carolina, and many others.

LEAD Kentucky. Although the District 180 Model/NCLB/SB1 required that principals of priority schools be replaced with a highly experienced, successful principal, often those people were not available, particularly in the rural areas. Given the philosophy of looking around to existing partnerships and those reaching out to Kentucky, the commissioner consulted with higher education and the Jefferson County superintendent (with 100,000 students, the largest district with the most priority schools) and pursued the National Institute for School Leadership to create a pilot to see if they could train the ER/university and local staff to become trainers for principals of priority schools.

The initial cohort involved key staff from Morehead State University, the University of Louisville, and Murray State, ER staff, and staff from Jefferson County. A PDSA was written to scale and spread the training. As of this writing, four hundred principals have been trained through LEAD Kentucky on turnaround best practice while building collegial relationships with principals in their regions to provide collaborative support.

U.S. Department of Education. Funding was and is an issue every year. ER staff is notified in April whether the department believes there will be money to pay them next year. Many are told to seek other employment even though there may be funding. As mentioned before, Donna Tackett had USDOE Title I and SIG offices on speed dial. She found that when we had all our documents aligned (NCLB waiver/SIG documents/title plans) with the desire of our hearts for how funding was to go toward college and career readiness for all students, permission could be granted.

It was seldom early or in enough time to spare anxiety but done nonetheless. Sometimes KDE personnel found particularly in the waiver phone calls that people from USDOE were not always aware of the Title I and SIG efforts being the same. In-house communication at all levels is key. That said, the USDOE often called on Kentucky to be a partner or provide information to other states.

Shipley and Associates. Jim Shipley and Associates (JSA), mentioned earlier for their systems documents, was already being called on by many districts and individual schools for continuous improvement training. The work of JSA is built on the education criteria of the Baldrige for performance excellence processes. Every time education recovery/KDE has asked for a collaborative ear or piloting use of materials, they have stepped up. Thinking collaboratively worked across agency offices too.

When the special education division was applying for a grant to rebuild the professional learning behind coteaching, one of the components added was continuous improvement classrooms. After all, that is what an individualized education plan is all about. So the process being used for response to intervention in priority schools was to be built into coteaching training. The people at Shipley assisted the department in building that component and providing training to trainers in each region for support.

Shipley has provided training for ER staff as requested. Although many of the specific Shipley tools can be and are purchased by districts, the concept of building to capacity and scale for continuous improvement is at best "random." Still, at least one regional cooperative has chosen to use Shipley as trainers and to provide the support mechanism for improving the districts in the cooperative.

In a telephone interview with David Johnson, former superintendent and now director of the Southeast/South Central Education cooperative, he was asked why the cooperative had sought out Shipley and Associates. Of course, the response was not as simple as that. Director Johnson shared that when he began as director after having been a superintendent in that cooperative, he knew they were frustrated at years of change. He had appreciated how the commissioner had been very direct about the importance of the work of District 180. Southeast/South Central did not have any priority schools at the time, but Director Johnson saw his role in the educational cooperative was to help the schools be successful.

Johnson decided that he would get in touch with the Kentucky Department of Education and find out what KDE was thinking and what resources they had that could help. He had to learn quickly that the terminology was very important and that everybody had to work together. Associate Commissioners Amanda Ellis and Foster helped with the discussion on alignment of resources. He made sure that communication of email, phone, and a novice reduction implementation through the department were followed.

Mr. Johnson noted that the school-level experience of both those associates and his experience as a superintendent assisted in understanding the needs of the cooperative. Mr. Johnson still believes there is much opportunity for cooperatives and KDE associates to dialogue on a conversational rather than workshop approach to ensure the needs and concerns of cooperatives are addressed.

The SESC cooperative's approach (there are eight cooperatives in the state and each works a little differently) was to help districts develop specific learning plans through a coaching model to build capacity. That gets us to Shipley and Associates.

As mentioned previously, there was already an initiative through the special education cooperatives called CT4GC (Co-Teaching for Gap Closure), which was proving to be successful in the areas that were taking the time and were committed to implementing it right and well. One of the components of that training was continuous classroom improvement. That team often used Shipley and Associates materials for that component. At this point in the discussion, Mr. Johnson deferred to Melissa Reynolds, who was responsible for the growth of that work in the cooperative. His parting word though was that districts are asking for the training rather than feeling that it is compliance now.

Melissa Reynolds was a practitioner in the field working with special education when she was tapped to coordinate this work at the SESC cooperative.

She has worked directly with the Shipley consultant in the CT4GC work. She had seen cooperative classrooms in which it was impossible to tell which teacher was the regular education teacher and which was the special educator.

Continuous improvement was the ticket. She began conversations with Cay Moore, the consultant in Kentucky for Shipley, who was training the trainers for continuous classroom improvement in the region. Training and implementation as they go takes three years. In 2017–18 there are to be model classrooms in the region for others to visit. This is the first three-year group in the cooperative. Other districts are at other stages of implementation.

Ms. Reynolds indicated that the first year was the toughest because a three-year commitment is hard for districts, schools, and teachers. Still, those who have made the commitment are seeing the difference in continuous improvement classrooms at all levels.

Continuous classroom improvement uses PDSA, data, Consensograms, goal setting, and other quality tools equipping and empowering students to own their own learning. Aligned with District 180 work and state work but not sponsored by KDE, this initiative in the Southeast/South Central Cooperative grew out of a need of the cooperative, an alert director, and a cooperative state department working with an ever flexible vendor. Ongoing training with education recovery staff and principals with JSA is a part of the quality check for fidelity of implementation of quality tools.

BUILDING A CULTURE OF CONTINUOUS IMPROVEMENT THROUGH APPLICATION OF SPECIFIC TOOLS (STATE AND LOCAL LEVEL) (APPENDIX F)

What It Is and Why It Is Needed

Once school team members identified their big rocks, how did they know what to do to get the information to write a 30-60-90-day plan that would be effective? The D180 model had a few requirements. There would be quarterly progress reporting to the state. The report would include attendance and updates on whatever goals the school/district SIG grant applications said would be monitored, which were primarily behavior interventions and math and literacy performance.

The format for the report evolved over time and is not included in this book as it will be adjusted to align with the Kentucky accountability model adopted in August 2017. The original component parts are still included. After submission of the reports, the ERDs met with the commissioner monthly to share progress and barriers.

The teams in the schools quickly realized that the way schools were organized was often a hindrance to the goals that had been set. In some schools, changes could be made quickly. In other schools, changes to the organizational structure would take much time. Still, the 30-60-90-day plan was a requirement. Data questions use was a requirement. The tools used to get the work done became vital to creating the learning environment needed in schools that would make the most progress.

KEY IDEAS

- The State Department must build an infrastructure for design and implementation of support for schools. For Kentucky these were:
  - Technology platform
  - Diagnostic review process: provide ongoing aligned information of desired systems/outcomes
  - Alignment of federal/state laws and regulations and requirements
  - Planning process: 30-60-90-day plans
  - System questioning
  - Professional learning communities
  - Improvement process PDSA
  - Two-way partnerships
  - Culture of continuous improvement through reporting

Chapter 7

Building a Culture of Continuous Improvement through Application of Quality Tools

Following are the key tools that were used. This writing, of course, is in hindsight. The design in 2010 did not include all the elements and tools that would emerge as needed for success. Agility and problem solving had to be core values to move forward.

TOOL 1: QUARTERLY REPORTS AND FEEDBACK (LOCAL FOR STATE)

What It Is

The quarterly report began as a series of charts in which monthly data would be reported by the schools to the educational recovery director. The report included progress on attendance and progress toward the school's big rocks. When the reports were submitted to the ERD or read at a regular visiting session with the school, the ERD would provide feedback to the schools regarding the quarterly report assessment.

This feedback was essential to create an effective action plan. The ERDs would summarize the reports and share that information with the commissioner and other state department people each quarter. The first report to the Kentucky Department of Education on actual data was not until the winter of 2013.

How It Was Used Effectively

Contributed by Carolyn Spangler (ERL)

In the beginning of the Lawrence County (LC) High School story, the quarterly report was deemed and completed as compliance. In the very early beginnings of our work in LC the feedback from the ERD, as well as the educational recovery team, usually was taken initially as a "to do list" by the LC administrators. Lawrence County High School (LCHS) and LC district-level leadership were not yet "fans" of the "turnaround" process or the requirements of the SIG, and were not yet believers in the tools/processes to be implemented or the ER team members' daily guidance and support.

LC leadership was all about "just tell us what you want us to do and we will do it"; they were not yet ready to see the quarterly report as a tool for continuous improvement. It would take at least a year and a half for the "dust" to settle from the required processes of being identified as a "persistently low-achieving" school to reveal the first "aha" moment of reckoning that would reveal the power within themselves to change the direction of their system.

As a former principal and current educational recovery leader I knew that compliance was a place to start. The ER team kept our message the same, the work ever before us focused on the tools, data, and guidance of the data questions to keep the coaching process on the use of tools/data/next steps instead of people, and eventually all eyes were on just that, the process.

The use of tools, data collection, and creating next steps became a unifier of the work: an organizational process that would bring about meaningful conversations among teachers and school- and district-level leadership. The processes became a collective work with the ER team as accepted support and trainers of the tools.

The principal would eventually set the tone with clear expectations of our collaborative work with the quarterly report, what pertinent information that was to be tracked, how often, who was responsible, why it was important, and alignment with SIG goals requirements, and from this moment we would begin building a system of data collection and reporting moving slowly but surely toward actions.

Our LC process became much like a flow chart, becoming a fluid flow of "how we were learning to do business." The principal assigned and disseminated data sets to appointed owners. In addition, he gave concrete due dates for the owners to ensure he and the ER team had time to analyze the information before the final submission of the report to the ERD.

Content teachers, specifically math/language arts, were to lead discussions of the data sets collected on formative assessments, measure of academic progress (MAP) data, failure data, and eventually response to intervention (RTI) data sets and how this process would "grow" the professional learning community (PLC) process with rich discussions, analyzing of data sets, recording progress within the PLC minutes, and submitting recorded notes to the principal with identified next steps. These were beginning stages of PLC protocol at a new level for LCHS.

Counselors' responsibilities, with principal direction, would have a new intentional and specific focus that included a laser focus on students who were on track in their career path, preparatory, college, and career ready, offering of career paths, KOSSA (Kentucky Occupational Skills Standards Assessment) testing, industry certification, etc., and would report as "owners" of these data sets of the quarterly report. The quarterly report demanded collection of nonacademic data sets such as attendance, drop out, behavior information, and safety information. The owners of these data sets were usually assistant principals.

Our LC process was that all quarterly report data set owners—teacher leaders, counselors, the principal, assistant principals—would submit their part of the quarterly report once they had reviewed and answered the data questions. This process ensured that the quarterly report was owned by the data owners and not by a district official. Before the ERD's firm due date, our LC team would conduct an administrative team meeting that included our district liaison support personnel and Chief Academic Officer Cassandra Webb.

The process that seemed to move our team clearly forward would be the use of the six data questions that were required at the end of each section of the quarterly report. Our quarterly leadership over time had to continue to strengthen and narrow their data-specific sets with percentages, point-to-distinct data, and then reveal their identified next step.

These data questions would lead us closer to real purposeful conversation about data usage instead of just data collectors. The data questions were required to be placed in the 30-60-90-day plan. Our overall quarterly analysis and collegial conversations would reveal what methodology was working and what was not working, were we getting the student achievement results we were after, and if not, what we were going to do about it.

All this information was collected at least two weeks before final submission on the first day of every third month, beginning on October 1. LCHS formalized administrative team meetings that included a district liaison, guidance counselors, assistant principals, teacher leaders, and ER team members would grow to have a second-layer administrative meeting with district-level personnel, which included the superintendent, CAO, DPP, finance officer, SPED, etc.

The principal and the ER team would be required to meet with the district-level administration, and the principal (as well as ER team members, if necessary) would lead the district-level team through the quarterly report and field questions. This second layer of reporting and analyzing would prove to be exceedingly beneficial in building a stronger understanding of the data usage of the quarterly tool as well as the 30-60-90-day planning and ultimately movement of student achievement. Support structures that were needed by the district to the school became increasingly identifiable. Our process became systematic, our data became more specific, and our next steps became clearer with each quarterly report process.

The superintendent (Mike Armstrong) began to require a quarterly report from each school, not just the priority high school. This process began to grow into the vision of including the LC Board of Education, a process created by the CAO (with full support of the superintendent). The quarterly report of each school would be presented at the regular LC BOE meeting by each building principal. Principals would report data and speak explicitly to the next steps that the principal would implement to ensure continuous student improvement and achievement.

Over time CAO Webb had the vision of training BOE members on the turnaround tools, such as the quarterly report, linkage, plus/delta, and data questions. The superintendent's support for this work was an allotment of one-hour working sessions before each regular Board of Education meeting. The training by the CAO empowered the LC BOE members and they soon asked detailed and knowledgeable questions of school-level leadership and/or district-level leadership about LC overall student achievement, improvement data, and processes to increase student achievement and success.

Quarterly reports were placed in BOE packets for the BOE members to review and analyze before the regular BOE meeting. The BOE members came to respect the quarterly data collection tool, reporting process, and the empowerment of the data questions and a continuous pulse of overall student performance on a quarterly basis. CAO Webb would prove to pave the way to critical, open communication among schools, districts, BOE members, and the LC community at large. She would become the visionary owner of the tools for turnaround and would lead the process. CAO Webb with superintendent support was the link among all leaders of the system.

It is imperative to note that the use of the required quarterly report and data questions were not used in isolation. The companion of the quarterly report would be a 30-60-90-day action plan of continuous improvement goals. From compliance of the LCHS PLA (bottom 5 percent) high school derived from the SIG to the adoption of district-wide use of the quarterly reporting process and the companion of the 30-60-90-day plan that became required of each school in LC, coupled with working sessions with the LC BOE before each regular board meeting, ultimately resulted in the development of the LC district data dashboard.

The development would include quarterly reporting on MAP data results district-wide. Quarterly reporting and access to 30-60-90-day plans reported systematically each quarter would result in a culture and climate shift, creating an atmosphere of informed conversations and questions that lead to action-specific steps with deadlines and high expectations. The positive gain in quarterly data student achievement would be the first "aha" reckoning that revealed to teachers/principals and administration at all levels of the LC system how all the tools/processes and protocols assisted them in seeing how all the pieces of the puzzle would fit together to bring about real systemic change.

It has been my experience that schools and districts are very good at collecting "data," but unfortunately that is the extent of their process. There is not a way for them to ask themselves if they are collecting the right data, nor are there systematic processes in which to see what is working, what is not working, where there is room for improvement, what there is to celebrate, and what our next steps are. Random data collection does not lead to use of tools of change, instructional processes, and/or identifying student-specific skill deficits of each individual student and ensuring support for that deficit.

Once our teachers at LC would see the student achievement needle move, we would slowly begin to meet in our PLCs with real purpose. Focus data sets were used to inform teachers about areas of instructional practice and methodology. Self-discovery of how to use data to move individuals and groups of students from this knowledge would grow purposeful, intentional RTI needs groupings of students and began to identify and address individual skill needs.

Teachers began to assist their students with personalized goal setting. Teachers could teach/coach students on what the student's MAP score really meant, Rauch Unit (rit) bands in language arts and math were explained to students, and students would set their own goals. When students realized that the universal screener (MAP) was important because they could be placed in a remedial class for math/language arts, they soon took note and took their individual MAP test with focus.

Over time the LC hallways would bolster students who met the benchmark in math, reading, or both. Students who were college ready, career ready, or both were celebrated throughout the school. The climate and culture of the entire building took on a new look and feel. Each classroom would proudly display data boards of student goals and achievements and students oversaw updating or moving the goals and targets. This process would bring about more student responsibility in their own learning.

I believe it was two years (maybe two and a half years) into the SIG turnaround process that the district-level leadership, PLA school-level leadership, and ER team became united in our combined efforts. They witnessed the identified PLA school not only exit priority status, but the district also began to embrace the turnaround process, tools, and ER support/guidance/ professional learning to ensure and "trickle down" the turnaround process throughout all LC feeder schools to the PLA high school. The Lawrence County High School principal would be deemed to have the capacity to lead the school in the turnaround process. Identified PLA school Leslie County would exit PLA status by year three; however, it would take LC four years to exit PLA status.

Compiled through an interview with Dr. Cassandra Webb (CAO Lawrence County Schools)

"'Oh no, not another state department person,' was my initial reaction when we learned in Lawrence County that we were one of the ten identified PLA schools." Lawrence County had been helped by the state since 1996. "We didn't really know what to expect with this new law or what it meant to be one of the ten. In fact, we found out through a press release!"

After their initial reaction, the feeling for Lawrence leadership was one of "embarrassment," according to Webb. Expressing skepticism at first, Webb realized after working with the ERD and ERL for a short time that they were not there to tell them what to do. Instead they were there to help them identify what Lawrence needed to do through use of common tools.

The big rock 30-60-90-day plan connected to system beliefs provided a backdrop for the improvements. Webb said the next major piece was to ensure that data and data questions were a regular piece of the work. The quarterly report became an extremely important part of the understanding of the work at all levels. Webb with the support of her superintendent built a district data room to monitor progress and report to the Board of Education.

Eventually Lawrence even set a standard higher than the state accountability requirements for themselves. Webb became the guardian of teams, data, and linkage charts and a leader in the deployment of all. She developed an instructional leader's team for the district based on the same principles and tools being used at the high school.

Now, seven years later, even with a different superintendent in the district, a visit to Lawrence would provide the visitor with evidence of continued use of the tools. The high school principal moved to a district position in another district. The new high school principal had been the assistant. At least three teachers from Lawrence County High School have become principals in other settings using lessons learned from the Lawrence journey.

"We realized that the answers were always within," reflects CAO Webb, now Dr. Webb, having received her EdD from Morehead State with a capstone from this work. "We had to come to terms that all of our systems were broken, and the fix would come through building sustainable structures one at a time. District 180 was a good thing for Lawrence. Being told you are the worst is an embarrassment and a motivator. We now own our own systems."

TOOL 2: SYSTEMS LINKAGE, SYSTEMS CHECKS, AND QUESTIONING SYSTEMS (STATE AND LOCAL) (EXAMPLES IN APPENDIX E)

What It Is

The systems linkage chart is a graphic organizer explaining the component parts of a system and the interaction of those parts. It is loosely based on the seven categories of the Baldrige criteria for performance excellence and is used to connect parts of a system together in the minds of the workers. It is used as an initial introduction to systems.

When It Was Used Effectively

Story I: Lawrence (Rural High School)

Contributed by Carolyn Spangler (ERL)

The educational recovery staffs in Leslie and Lawrence would be the first students that Susan Allred would introduce/train on the Baldrige criteria for performance excellence systems. The expectation was that each of the three-member teams was not only to learn but to be users of the systems linkage, systems check, and questioning protocols.

I will not soon forget that as ERD, Allred wryly explained to me that as the ERL I was the leader of the educational recovery team, that if the turnaround process/SIG requirements were not implemented, my "head would be the first to roll"! Clearly our team learned the required systems well and worked diligently to ensure that the three of us were working as a team. If we understood our clearly defined roles and could do a pulse check on how we were doing as a team, we could be model leaders of teamwork.

We would soon begin to train the administrators and the teachers on the Baldrige-based linkage system. The ERL worked specifically with administrators, principals, assistant principals, counselors, and librarians. The ER specialists worked with teachers to introduce, teach, and lead them in the creation of their own linkage charts. The linkage would be reviewed quarterly and became part of our administrative team meetings.

ERD Allred would be the first to introduce the Baldrige-based linkage team system process to LC administrators, which included a special education

director, finance officer, director of pupil personnel, and chief academic officer. Each director would create his or her own individual linkage chart, and
ERD Allred would review at the next monitoring visit. Special Education
Director Rhonda Colvin made the connection to the linkage system immediately. She would prove to be an advanced systems thinker. Thus began the
very first LC system to undergo an "overhaul," a restructuring based on data
sets that indicated the current system was not being effective. In fact, it was
broken.

Getting started to implement the design changes into practical work was the
work of the ERL, special education director, and LC administration to using
a PIA (Plan, Inquire, Act like PDSA) tool from Harvard to determine the root
cause and action needed. The ERL demonstrated the PIA process using the
plan, inquire, and act to begin our conversations as a unified ER team/district-
level team to dig into a problem with the special education system.

The work included data tracking, identification, folders, folder review process, Infinite Campus (state data system) issues, and comprehensive scrutiny
of all data sets for special education students with assistance from the ERD
and ERL, as needed. SPED Colvin would prove her systematic thinking in
reorganizing her process/protocol structures and conduct intentional and specific professional learning with her teachers/training, constantly using the
continuous improvement process to ensure a clearly defined systematic process for each of her "spokes" of the special education system wheel.

SPED Colvin would go on to present her linkage systems understanding in
other districts. She would become a "go to" person for her improved systematic district-wide special education system that ran like a well-oiled machine,
all spokes turning the giant wheel of special education in Lawrence County.
Each time ERD Allred came to LC for monitoring, review, and support of the
district and school, she worked specifically with Special Education Director
Colvin and Chief Academic Officer Cassandra Webb on linkage/systems/pro-
cess and protocols of their assigned roles/responsibilities with the LC system

At each visit to the district-level leadership central office for administrative
meetings, etc., all could see linkage charts by each of the director's desks.
*Personal note from Spangler: This would bring a smile to my face because
I knew that ERD Allred had led the work with the district leadership and had
set clear expectations of usage. The process would prove as another con-
nector of the school and district work as the LC administration and teachers
had their linkage charts posted for all to see. I knew the two connections
would soon come together in time. A very wise ERD kept telling this ERL,
"It takes the time it takes." I would soon witness the truth of the statement in
Lawrence County as well as other assigned schools and districts throughout
my career.*

The expansion to our work would come with a relationship development between CAO Webb and the ERL. A trust began to build that would allow us to work closely, collaboratively, honestly, and, more important, systematically toward the overall improvements of the LC system. The turning point in my personal and professional opinion came with CAO Webb requesting a meeting with the ERL and within that meeting she said with great heart and painful passion, "Carolyn, all of our systems are broken." It was here that we agreed to work on one system at a time, together.

The door was finally open for the ERL to train and work with principals at principal meetings on linkage, team systems check, and the developing of the big seven days of professional learning, (a vision of CAO Webb) that would prove to turn the ship of academic achievement of the Lawrence County School System. The ERL would work with district-wide counselors and FRYSC (Kentucky Family Resource and Youth Service Center) personnel on linkage/team systems check. ER specialists would work with teachers throughout the district.

There it was, an entire district unified and working with ER team members. An observer would not be able to tell the local LC staff from the "state people." Such a time is important because for the very first time they were a team. The district was becoming a team with clearly defined communication channels, roles, and responsibilities, along with standards and data-specific training. One voice now. One Lawrence County owning the work from this point forward.

What the linkage tool would do for the Lawrence County District was reveal a need for more than an organization chart. There was a need for individual understanding of purpose and unique service to the LC school district. The linkage tool and team systems check would soon be discussed at the district-level meetings, and leaders would have meaningful conversations on how each person was connected to the other person and how each job relied on another job linked to the LC System.

Over time all positions in the district were defined by a linkage chart. It could be a bus driver or maintenance director, but regardless, each person in LC understood his or her importance to his or her clear, defined role and his or her responsibility in the success of the Lawrence County School System. This continuous improvement process has developed over time with consistent, persistent, and diligent efforts to stay the course of a unified team—"All in LC," a phrase coined by the current superintendent (Dr. Robbie Fletcher), most likely explains the purpose best.

CAO Webb, with support from the superintendent, continues to refine and improve LC systems and processes. The linkage on the wall at LC now represents the comprehensive district improvement plan (CDIP) goals that are aligned and collapsed into one document with common goals of continuous student achievement and success. Lawrence County has welcomed many guests to observe their "living linkage wall" process. The district has been deemed a proficient district and the LCHS was named a distinguished school; however, neither district nor high school is satisfied. They continue to re-define success and are encouraged by the discovery of the power within, the power of team.

Story II: Fleming Linkage Example (Rural District and High School)
Contributed by Julia Rawlings (ERS, ERL, ERD)

In the fall, the education recovery director conducted a systems linkage training for the Fleming County High School administrative team consisting of the principal, assistant principal, curriculum coach, two guidance counselors, two ERSs, and the ERL. This training was part of a series of trainings on a systems approach to continuous improvement, focusing specifically on systems integration through linkage. During this training, the first goal was to ensure that all members of the leadership team had a clear, common understanding of their organization regarding communication, organiza-tional values, and monitoring performance expectations around the needs of students, staff, and the larger community.

At this point, the members of the leadership team moved around a series of posters that posed a variety of questions related to each of the seven cat-egories: leadership, strategic planning, customer focus, management analysis and knowledge management, workforce focus, process management, and finally results. As they moved through these seven categories, each person put sticky notes on the chart paper to respond to the questions individually. After all questions on all seven chart papers were responded to, they revisited each poster with responses as a group to discuss and develop a shared under-standing of each category based on leadership team member responses.

This process allowed the team, collectively, to develop a common under-standing to complete each category of the school linkage chart. Once the school linkage chart was completed, each individual or job-alike group (for example, principal, assistant principal, counselors) completed the process again to complete their own individual or job-alike linkage chart. As part of the conclusion of the training, each member of the leadership team was asked to reflect on the previous day's activities by listing them separately on a sticky note.

The facilitator then posted the completed school linkage chart from earlier in the day and asked each participant, one at a time, to come to the linkage chart to put the sticky note of each activity in the appropriate category on the linkage chart where it was directly related. This became a very reflective event as each member had to determine if the activity was directly related and would have an impact on the ultimate results they had identified on the linkage chart.

The team discussed each sticky note placement as it related to the category and the person's own linkage chart. Each member repeated this process until we had a linkage chart full of sticky notes representing the previous day's work in that school. As the leadership team members completed this activity, the facilitator conducted a discussion of the role each person had in contributing to the linkage chart: the goals, student and staff performance, data, qualification requirements of the workforce, processes used, and results.

The final activity was to address the sticky notes that didn't seem to fit any category and were stuck outside the linkage chart categories. The facilitator asked a series of questions about each activity to get participants to understand how the activities they did daily either contributed to school goals or not.

Questions included:

- Were the activities outside their scope of work?
- Were the activities actually someone else's responsibility but were being micromanaged by that participant?
- Was it a necessary activity?
- How can this activity be conducted differently to contribute to the goals of the school?

This final activity was very impactful to the effectiveness of the leadership team as they realized how each member contributed to the goals of the school, the scope of the work that each member was responsible for doing, and how, collectively, they work together to achieve the goals of the school.

The plus/delta that was completed at the end of the day was full of pluses and a few thoughtful deltas that included things like: What do we do next as a team to ensure we are on track with our own work as it contributes to the goals of the school? How can I eliminate activities in my day that do not fit on the linkage chart? How can we ensure that the school and individual linkage is shared with staff?

As the final step, the facilitator asked that each delta be addressed with a next step. It was determined by the leadership team that they would conduct a "standing meeting" each morning at 7:20 a.m. to replicate the posting of sticky notes activity and discuss how they could work more effectively and efficiently that day to achieve their individual and school goals as well as identify specific times when each linkage chart would be revisited to determine if adjustments were needed.

The school continues to faithfully complete their standing meetings before school begins each day.

Story III: Pulaski Linkage Example (Rural High School)

Contributed by Todd Tucker (ERL)

My journey as an educational recovery leader was one that began with limited sustainable success. My experience in school turnaround leadership included doing what I would label as educational best practice "stuff." I was always trying to "fix" the people within the schools instead of fixing the school system that currently was not supporting the students and teachers. Reviewing data from identified priority schools, it was evident that priority schools implementing a systems approach to improvement were being more successful in their transformation efforts.

I wanted to learn more about this approach. I was provided an opportunity to participate in several trainings on the systems approach. However, it didn't resonate with me until a colleague who was mentored in the systems approach met with me during a diagnostic review of the school I was supporting. She told me that several good things were going on at the school. However, it was the recovery staff doing the work. We were driving the continuous improvement efforts. We were doing lots of educational best practice "stuff" to "fix" the people.

The linkage chart that had been shared with me on several occasions began making sense. I realized for transformation efforts to work and become sustainable, I had to become effective in applying leadership skills, strategies, and tools to engage the stakeholders of the school in taking ownership of the transformation process. My role was to work strategically with the leadership team to develop systems to support students and teachers.

For me this meant working above the line in the linkage chart. My goal was to work with the school's leadership to set strategic direction and to develop an improvement plan that focused on identified needs. The "below the line" operational section would be where the teachers and students implement the systems developed by the leadership team to accomplish the improvement efforts.

This systems approach was one that engaged staff in taking ownership of the transformation process and helped ensure improvement efforts would continue once state assistance was no longer provided to the school.

TOOL 3: PLUS/DELTA (LOCAL AND STATE) (EXAMPLE IN APPENDIX E)

What It Is

There is no shortage of opinions in education. Depending on the experience level, understanding, attitude, general knowledge, and information of the stakeholders/workers at any given time, meetings can be endless. To conserve time as well as to get all the information from everyone equally, the plus/delta tool was used almost 100 percent of the time to gather information on plus (what is working or going well) and delta (what needs to change). Sometimes there would also be a recommendations section for how to address the deltas.

The key to gathering information this way is that at the next meeting of the group or through electronic means all the items are reviewed through use of the data questions. People are hesitant at first but over time, when they see the results used, the plus/delta becomes a very important tool for buy-in and improvement for building a collaborative culture.

It was to be used and was used at every level by all system leaders within the school.

How It Was Used Effectively

Contributed by Jeanne Crowe (ERL) (rural high school)

East Carter High School (ECHS) found the plus/delta tool to be invaluable in our continuous improvement efforts. The plus/delta serves as a great communication instrument between staff and leadership (faculty meetings, leadership team meetings, and professional learning communities, etc.) to gauge staff concerns, culture and climate target areas, professional learning opportunities, and effectiveness along with providing an overall status of the school. Deltas are always addressed, which is critically important in building relationships and trust.

Additionally, the plus/delta was integrated into the classroom and into the student data notebooks. After a summative assessment, end of unit, or even periodic student checks (plus/delta charts on back doors and sticky notes as students leave the classroom), teachers would use the tool to gather student feedback. This facilitates instructional decisions in meeting student needs, reflection on teacher practice, and provides insight into the daily classroom setting. This tool has contributed to staff and student ownership of the great things occurring at ECHS both academically and culturally.

Recognized as one of the three Kentucky hub schools, ECHS also uses the plus/delta with our visitors from across the state to gain outside perspective on our systems and to continue improving. Each district/school visiting team can do Q&A with our student panel. This idea stemmed from a plus/delta desiring to have time to talk more with students. These discussions are always a favorite part of the day with our visitors. Another idea came from a delta requesting a list of resources each content area uses, which we have now created for sharing.

The plus/delta is a systems tool that is used not only in our school and our district but also throughout our state. When I ask our visitors to complete the plus/delta, most are quick to say they are familiar with or have used this tool. The value has widespread recognition and has implications in so many areas of the educational environment

Necessary Resources

The plus/delta is another tool that we like and use because it is free. Leadership must model this practice always and provide feedback for it to be successful.

TOOL 4: THE TELL KENTUCKY SURVEY (STATE-LEVEL SUPPORT, LOCAL USE)

What It Is

To determine teacher perceptions of climate and working conditions, every two years since 2011 the Teaching, Empowering, Leading, and Learning (TELL) Kentucky survey has been administered to receive feedback from administrators, principals, counselors, and teachers on the following topics:

- Community Engagement and Support
- Teacher Leadership
- School Leadership
- Managing Student Conduct
- Use of Time
- Professional Development
- Facilities and Resources
- Instructional Practices and Support
- New Teacher Support

Although intended for all schools and districts, the voluntary survey is encouraged in District 180 schools by using the data to improve working conditions. Working conditions can easily be one of the three big rocks in a 30-60-90-day planning process if the TELL survey has been responded to in sufficient numbers to show a trend. Since 2013, 100 percent of the priority schools have participated and in most of the schools 100 percent of staff within those schools have participated.

The New Teacher Center provides analysis on a statewide basis and provides a special report on responses from District 180 schools to assist decision makers in District 180 with working conditions in priority schools and help them build support systems for principals in those settings.

How It Was Used Effectively

Contributed by Julia Rawlings (ERS, ERL, ERD) (rural high school)

East Carter High School was identified in the 2010–11 school year as a persistently low-achieving school; additionally, this was also the year for administration of the TELL Kentucky survey. Because this was a working conditions survey, the administration really communicated the value of the results and what they could do to improve their current working conditions at the school. Morale was very low at this point because of their recent label of PLA. The staff did value the survey. There was a 100 percent survey completion rate from all certified staff in the building.

Upon receiving the TELL Kentucky data, the principal shared and analyzed the data with the staff and administrators. The administrative team (comprised of the principal, assistant principal, guidance counselor, and ER team) took the next steps to truly disaggregate the data as a school. After the administration disaggregated the data, each department went through this same process in their departmental PLCs. The disaggregation used by both groups included the use of the data questions to determine the next steps for the school as well as each department. It was very important that each department had a voice in what they felt the next steps should be.

One area that was identified by all departments and the administration was the area of professional development (PD), in which teachers were asked to rate how strongly they agree or disagree with statements such as "professional development is differentiated to meet the needs of individual teachers." It was overwhelmingly the lowest area of agreement within the entire TELL Kentucky survey with only 24.6 percent of the staff agreeing that their PD was meeting their individual needs.

Because each department had done its own disaggregation and completed the data questions, the team was able to quickly create their 30-60-90-day plan around the year's professional development offerings. One of the first steps in the thirty-day plan was to have each department complete a needs assessment of their own individual and departmental professional development needs. These needs assessments were then used by the administrative team to develop a PD plan for each department that included both job-embedded and day-long professional development offerings to meet their needs. Each department had very specific needs that were both pedagogical and content area in nature, which made identification of in-district/in-house and outside presenters quite difficult.

As the year progressed, each area of the 30-60-90-day plan had been addressed to meet the needs of individual teachers as evidenced by the plus/deltas, PD surveys, and PLC meetings. Meeting individual teacher professional development needs has continued to be a focus to ensure that all staff are equipped to provide effective learning environments.

The results of the biannual survey continue to have increased levels of agreement from staff, moving from 24.6 percent in 2011 to 63.6 percent in the most recent TELL Kentucky administration in March 2017. An additional survey question, "At this school, we utilize the results from the TELL Kentucky survey as a tool for school improvement," increased levels of agreement from staff, moving from 73.3 percent in 2013 (first administration of this question) to 80.4 percent in 2015 and is at 87.5 percent in 2017 (Kentucky TELL Survey, 2011 and 2017).

Necessary Resources

The survey is administered in alternating years and used for goals throughout the two-year period until it is administered again. As of 2017, Title II federal funds currently on the chopping block for the federal budget have provided this invaluable resource. When the data is used over the entire period, it is most valuable.

TOOL 5: INDIVIDUAL AND GROUP TEACHER SUPPORT JUST IN TIME (ALL LEVELS)

What It Is

In anyone's career, it is important to have support at the moment one needs it to move to the next level of improvement. That is true no matter the level. Take the two of us, for example.

On a personal note (Foster): After working as a building principal and district instructional supervisor for ten years, I was starting to feel like I was a paper pusher and that I was disconnected from instruction. I decided to apply to be an HSE so I could have a more direct role in teacher and leadership development. Lucky for me this career move would lead me to meeting Susan Allred and Dr. Holliday. This is when "doing the work" became more about "developing a system for the work" to occur. They were the support I needed just in time.

And Susan: On completing my education specialist's degree in 1989 at Appalachian State University I was encouraged by my professors to pursue my doctorate. ASU did not have a program. My specific interest was teacher support. I had read much of Dr. William Purkey's (UNC–Greensboro) work around invitation to education and decided that was where I would apply. After I was denied entrance into the program because I was not "focused sufficiently for the program," I decided instead to focus on teacher support as a school administrator.

Good choice for me because I would meet Dr. Holliday within the month. The lesson learned is that doors of support close and open in education just in time. Period. Don't give up. The door that closed might limit you to the known. The unknown is very fulfilling. There is plenty of work to do. Just in time support is needed no matter who we are!

No matter if it is Dr. John Hattie's effect size, metacognitive studies of effectiveness, Dr. Robert Marzano's research on instructional strategies, or almost any university's educational bodies of research on classroom practices, teachers matter. Our own observation regarding teachers in Kentucky is that they care passionately about the students they teach.

Kentucky is a teacher unionized state. In most of the work around priority schools, the local negotiating units have been supportive of adjustments that needed to be made to move student performance forward. Sometimes the road has been rocky as legal language is resolved, but the teachers themselves, once they understand and own the idea that they can make a difference, are absolutely on board.

It is a slow process to move high schools from the idea of each person as an individual contractor who teaches a specific discipline/subject to all of us are responsible for all the students in this building. The thinking is different, and few educators have been trained to be collaborators in effective teams. They are good at what they do individually but not necessarily together.

Teachers in any given building seldom were graduates of the same teacher education programs and the programs are different at each university. Particularly in small rural districts, the central offices do not have sufficient staff to coordinate effective common instructional practices training or provide individual support for teachers who struggle. When a school is extremely low performing, often teachers have learned to survive in the environment. They often have great hearts but have lost the joy of the possibilities.

District 180 and state involvement were not welcomed with open arms in those first years but rather with a cautious skepticism of any help. Some of the initial ten schools had received assistance since the 1990 KERA legislation. So what approach would the coaches need to take with the school-based staff?

Armed with the concept of 30-60-90-day plans and quarterly reporting, the ERS staff began to work with the math and literacy teachers to build instructional systems for success. Of course, this works only if the ERS totally understands his or her role as to what he or she can and must do and how to work with adults. Success is not promised. The early TELL surveys would indicate that teachers may have been very pleased with their schools and administrators before becoming priority and far less the year they were identified as priority and the ER team came to the school. The TELL data was one way to begin addressing those issues.

Susan Greer, who is currently an education recovery director and working with novice reduction at the state level, was an ERL at Leslie High School in 2010. When asked what she believes are the pieces that teachers must embrace if true systemic, systematic, and continuous improvement is to occur, she indicated:

- They must embrace a growth mindset versus a fixed mindset (Carol Dweck's work introduced to ER teams in training summer of 2011).
- They must work in teams instead of being independent contractors.
- They must develop the ability to see the big picture and then the concrete with incremental steps to achieve it.
- They must focus on skills and deficits of individual students rather than on grading. This is especially true where response to intervention works.
- They must be able to see themselves as part of an organization with common goals.
- They must build relationships with students to empower them (not just make assignments).

Example of Where It Worked Effectively

Contributed by Julia Rawlings (ERS, ERL, ERD) (mid-sized rural)

In the spring of 2011, the leadership assessment results were delivered to Carter County Schools and East Carter High School. The district was found to have the capacity to lead the school turnaround, but the school leader was found not to have the capacity. The school-based decision-making council lacked the capacity to support the turnaround work. When school leaders are found not to have capacity, they are removed from that position, so East

Carter High School would be searching for a new principal for the 2012–13 school year.

It was obvious that the school needed a leader much different from the one that had been in place for several years, one that would be able to effectively implement strategies to correct the deficiencies identified in the leadership assessment report. Mr. Larry Kiser, the current assistant principal at ECHS, was hired and started the position in July 2012.

Mr. Kiser had a very large and daunting task in front of him being a first-time principal: bringing life and success back to a building that had been failing in all aspects of the school environment (for example, academic, nonacademic, culture, climate) for at least the previous three years. His first month as the principal was like drinking water from a fire hose led by a leadership assessment report that identified the major deficiencies within the building, TELL Kentucky working conditions results, a school improvement grant (SIG) that needed major revisions, and a weeklong PLA school training—all of this with part-time ER support from one person at the time.

It became clear very quickly that Principal Kiser had to reflect and determine what his vision was for ECHS—how would he move it forward, who were the key players to help him, and how could he rally the broken troops around him. He knew that his leadership and vision could not look or feel like the previous principal's vision. Kiser's vision emerged from thoughtful reflections: they are the three Rs (Relationships, Relevance, and Rigor) and they had to be in that order!

He wanted relationships to be first and foremost: positive and powerful relationships between teachers and students, but also relationships among teachers (realize that not everyone wanted to see the former principal removed, which left cliques within the teaching and administrative staff). He understood the value of the staff being together in the work—everyone rowing in the same direction for the same reason.

His second vision requirement was that of relevant work for teachers and students (teachers must know why they are doing what they are being asked to do, just like kids must know). He also fully understood that failing student achievement scores had to be addressed. His solution was to ensure rigor of instruction happening in every classroom every day. Mr. Kiser modeled these daily as he worked with faculty, staff, students, parents, and community members.

The school's work became about those three big pieces of his vision and how they played a part in the work to be done (for example, SIG, 30-60-90-day plans, quarterly reports, school improvement plans, PLCs). He knew he could not do this alone, so with the help of the assistant principal, guidance counselors, instructional coach, and the ERL, he developed a plan to form a leadership team consisting of a representative of each content area (core, arts and humanities, and practical living/career studies), special education, the school administrative staff, and the district superintendent (new to the district assuming the council authority because capacity had been removed from the council).

Inviting the superintendent to attend these meetings could have gone down a bad path but it turned out to be a very positive one that led to very positive changes throughout the district. The charge of this group was to act as advisors to help make decisions that were best for the school. The leadership team became the sounding board for the principal weekly. This leadership team became a big part of the success of ECHS—they now had a voice they'd never had before, and it was having an impact on culture, climate, and student achievement.

Additional data collected biannually through the TELL Kentucky working conditions survey also indicated the change in overall working conditions (my school is a good place to work and learn) increased the agreement percentage from 70.5 percent in 2011 to 89.1 percent in 2013, 89.5 percent in 2015, and 93.3 percent in 2017 (TELL Kentucky Survey).

For the ERS staff to make things happen they must have a specific strategies toolbox to be successful. Schools and teachers do not have common belief systems of how schools should work. The strategies toolbox assisted ER team members in providing transformational support. Among those tools were common assessments, interventions, classroom coaching modeling, focused intentional organization of the work, relationship building to empower visionary leadership, teacher buy-in, and district support. Mr. Kiser had just in time support every day from the ERL and her toolbox.

Strategy for Use of Tools—Just in Time Support for Common Assessments: The Progression of Common Formative Assessments at Franklin Simpson High School

Contributed by Crystal White (ER) (rural, western part of the state)

During the summer prior to establishing common formative assessments, the leadership team at Franklin Simpson High School attended a weeklong training at its local co-op on how to collect and analyze data in the classroom using the five-step data analysis process. This was used as the preliminary data analysis tool at FSHS but soon morphed into much more sophisticated, time-saving, and teacher-driven methods.

The establishment of common formative assessments really began with the formation of PLCs, at least the first attempts at authentic PLCs for data collection and analysis to improve instruction within the classroom.

Previously, there had been no data analysis aside from state testing scores, which of course occurred well after the fact. We created with the following expectations:

- They were held with common content partners: ninth-grade ELA teachers made up a PLC, biology teachers made up a PLC, etc.
- They occurred on a regular schedule every two weeks.
- The purpose of "collecting data to drive instruction for improvement" was communicated and discussed.
- A protocol for each PLC meeting was introduced and explained.
- PLC partners were given time to set their norms after modeling had occurred.
- A monitoring and support schedule was set for administrators.

At the same time, during weekly guided planning sessions, which might be termed "embedded PD," formative assessments were introduced as to what they are, what they are not, why use them, etc. The natural progression from there was the introduction of common formative assessments among common content partners to drive conversations regarding improved instruction, assessment, and differentiation in PLCs.

Conversations were occurring during weekly guided planning sessions about standards, writing student-friendly learning targets, writing summative assessments that reflected the rigor of the standards, etc., and the leadership team began coaching. Through guided planning sessions, teachers were introduced to the idea of the collection and analysis of data to provide the next steps and interventions in the classroom. During a day-long learning community day (LCD), leadership introduced the five-step data analysis process learned the previous summer. The process was modeled by leadership and then practiced by PLC partners with guidance and support of the leaders. At the end of the LCD, PLCs presented their data to their department and discussion occurred as to what the data meant and what the next steps might be in the classroom.

At the end of that LCD the principal set the new PLC expectation that one of two things would be happening during PLCs, and they would alternate every other week:

1. PLCs would be creating common formative assessments (CFA) based on two or three standards in the unit currently being taught. CFAs would contain at least twelve to fifteen questions divided as evenly as possible among the standards.

2. PLCs would analyze and discuss the data from the most recent CFA and plan the next steps for intervention, as well as make changes to improve future instruction.

Quickly, some PLC teams began to use computer programs to create and save data for analysis. The less "techy" groups remained with the five-step process. However, after one teacher implemented the use of GradeCam with its ability to be synced with Infinite Campus, assign a standard to each question, and provide instantaneous data with graphics and individual students' progress, the principal purchased GradeCam for the school. He then empowered the teachers with prior experience to train the rest of the faculty on the use of GradeCam to manage and analyze data.

Please know that this was a two- to three-year process. The school used multiple protocols as teachers became more and more proficient in their analysis and discussions. After five years, teachers can be observed huddled up at their computer screens "PLCing" nearly every day during their planning periods, discussing data, instruction, and future planning. While a specific time has been carved into the weekly schedule for PLCs, nearly all common content partners work together each day.

Interventions

From an Interview with Kevin Gay (Principal, Leslie County High School, ERL) (very rural in Eastern Kentucky)

Kevin Gay had been principal for a little over a year and was determined through the leadership assessment to have capacity to lead Leslie County High School at the time of its designation as a PLA school. "We had to learn first that it isn't about buying programs to address the learning needs. There is no silver bullet intervention program." Already he had through his own modeling shown teachers that special needs students belonged to them. Already he was engaging students in determining the mission and vision of the school. Already he was building a learning culture. When the three-member ER team arrived in Leslie, they became a part of the larger leadership team that included key teachers and the counselors.

Gay indicated that what the ER team did was introduce quality tools, use of data, and used the PDSA and building PLCs that would drive interventions. They realized very quickly that core instruction had to be addressed before they could look far into interventions. Students and teachers started data notebooks.

By having the expanded leadership team there were sufficient people to attend all the PLCs to ensure the agenda was followed and that instruction was the key focus. The team then began to make decisions about an additional intervention period. Principal Gay looked at the school schedule and removed fifteen-minute student breaks, extended the day, and created a daily thirty-five-minute intervention period in language arts and math based on the performance data of students.

The role of counselors at this point cannot be overstated. The strong counselors (Mary Feltner and Robert Roark) as a part of the team changed schedules without flinching. Often. Teachers were required to teach skills and concepts based on the gaps. Individual and teacher data notebooks tracked effectiveness. "Ultimately," Gay points out, "we found out with the kids that they were the ones who had to own the data for this to work." By hands-on engagement of every leadership team member, support for the teachers in the intervention time, and kids buying in, the apparent chaos equaled learning!

After Leslie became the first of the priority schools to exit the designation, Kevin Gay became an ERL at other schools to help them know about how Leslie did it and how they can. This of course brings up the question: Why would you take the principal out of the school? It really is simple. The leadership team was so strong that they had a person to take his place. Leslie County High hadn't missed a beat. As a matter of fact, in July 2017, a former education recovery specialist from that 2010 team was named superintendent of Leslie County Schools, Linda Rains.

Classroom Coaching/Modeling

Contributed by Kim Cornett (ERL) with Debra Reed (ERL)

Every educational recovery specialist had the freedom to use strategies and tools that they had used before to be successful. The chart below was developed by Kim and Debra as a composite of the coaching tools they had in their personal toolboxes which were most helpful to them.

Focused Intentional Organization of the Work

From a Conversation with Mike Murphy (Principal Pulaski High School, ERL) and Tim Godbey (Principal, Lincoln County High School, ERL, ERD) (rural, South Central)

Mike Murphy and Tim Godbey were principals in priority schools. The topic was to be about meetings they held with their high school staffs, but they took it a bit deeper. Both men were moved to the principalship of the high schools as they went into PLA status. The schools were very different in what they needed from the start. The leadership styles of the two men had

Table 7.1 Coaching Strategies for Teacher Support

PLC Protocol Built around PDSA (DuFour Questions)	*Note: The PLC process is based on the current professional needs of teachers and evolves around specific needs as the team matures.
Classroom Observations	Observation tools may vary based on the purpose of the walkthrough (ELEOT, PGES, school-developed instruments). A coteaching walkthrough instrument was also used.
Unit/Lesson Rubric and Feedback Sessions	Used to set the expectation for the instructional process that was a consistent school-wide practice.
Modeling Instructional Strategies/Activities	Monthly provided support for teachers to implement in the classroom, monitored through principal observations.
Teacher-Led Professional Development	Developing teacher leaders to create a collaborative environment.
Learning Walks	Teachers observe best practice followed by a debriefing session.
Incorporate the Use of Quality Tools	Plus/delta, Consensograms, data-wise questions.
Curriculum Compacting Sessions	Provides teachers the opportunity to meet and strategically "chunk" content.
Transparent Communication	Provides informative feedback to increase instructional capacity. An emphasis was placed on understanding the "big picture" and how teachers contribute (linkage). Another example for transparent communication was board member working sessions when teachers and students organized stations to help board members understand relevant pieces of work (student data notebooks, RTI, strategies, etc.).
Monitoring Professional Growth Plans	Teachers developed action steps for professional growth plans and determine instructional next steps from walkthrough data.
New Teacher Support Structure	New teacher cadre and/or mentoring system.
Redefined Roles of Instructional Aides	Expectations and roles and responsibilities were redefined to encourage aides to become more active participants in the instructional process. Instructional aides are active members in the PLC process.
Building Relationships	Develop a "trust" with teachers to enable coaching to occur.
30-60-90-Day Plan	Provides an opportunity for teachers to set a goal and plan incrementally to reach it.
Quarterly Report	A data dashboard keeping teachers informed of the current state of the school in relation to attaining goals.
Data Walls/Data Notebooks	Used to monitor school-wide and individual student data pieces; fostering "coproducers of learning"; student-led conferences.

| Develop Teacher Leaders | PLC leads training on how to lead instructionally and facilitate meetings. |
| Professional Development | Identify PD needs of school/teachers, provide training, create implementation plan, monitoring plan. |

to be very different to get to the concept of coordination and alignment of meetings.

On the day of the interview Mike Murphy walked up to me, shook my hand, introduced himself, and said, "I just want to thank you for what you told me the first time we met." Personally, I did not remember the first time and looked a bit puzzled. "You came to Pulaski and were in the room with the district and school leaders, but out of that whole room you looked at me and told me that the former principal was removed because he didn't get the job done. Then you told me that I had two years, or I would be gone too." Wow. I said that? He went on to tell me that from there he had his marching orders for getting the work done at Pulaski High.

Mike described his leadership as "very pyramid in form." He indicated that there were many processes for safety and security of the environment he had to address. When he met the education recovery trio assigned to his building, he said that the ERL became his right hand and that the team was the initial leadership team of the school. A 30-60-90-day plan was written based on the data. He as principal told the staff they would do it. So initially the meetings were information to begin to build systems. Quick wins began to happen in both the safety and academic areas, which enabled staff and students to see it was a new day. Slowly but surely staff team meetings were built into the process.

Tim Godbey at Lincoln was also a first-year principal. He knew that Lincoln County High was a laughingstock and that could only be addressed with a full team effort. The education recovery team assigned guided them quickly into a 30-60-90-day plan and "hit the ground running." The 30-60-90-day plan was the driver of every day. He indicated that the first plan was weak, but it was the plan of the school as they understood the work at the time. He enjoyed watching the staff and the plan grow over a three-year period there to where now it is just the way they do work.

One of the key elements for Lincoln moving forward was celebrations for the right reasons: student and staff accomplishments. He vividly remembers a student telling him that the problem was that "nobody around here cares." The celebrations began to be a regular part of the caring process at Lincoln. Another tool he used with the leadership team at Lincoln was a ten-minute check-in every morning. Building agility into the daily work helped staff and students know the importance of every day. As staff became empowered, meetings were based on need. He said that he still had to handle daily issues.

Both Pulaski and Lincoln exited priority status. Different schools. Different structures. Different leadership styles. They both agreed there were some common leverages in addition to the ER tools. They were

a) the Kentucky accountability model establishing college and career readiness for all students as a directive,
b) the education recovery teams equipped with experience and tools,
c) the district being given a leadership assessment in addition to the school, meaning they were part of the issues and solutions, and
d) the school improvement grant (SIG) providing funding to implement and ensure sustainable systems being built.

Relationship Building to Empower Visionary Leadership, Teacher Buy-In, and District Support

From a Conversation with Kim Cornett (ERL), Debra Reed (ERL), Crystal White Higgins (ERS), and Jeanne Crowe (ERS)

"Out of all the things you do as educational recovery staff, how do you make it happen at the school level?" The responses in common of this group were building trust through transparency, respect, good communication of what was happening, and helping them see quick wins with student attendance, behavior, and achievement. Debra Reed added very quickly, "It really can't happen if the ER team doesn't have the building and district leadership support." Having worked full time in three PLA schools and supporting others, Debra would know.

The leadership view of the team and whether the team is there to help and can help is crucial. Another important piece this ERS group revealed is getting staff opinions and input to help staff realize their own value and importance in the work at hand. ERSs were not there just to listen but also to help staff see how to address those areas that concern them or understand why those concerns are not being addressed yet.

The ERS staff agreed that they had to get in the classroom with teachers in a professional manner to help them work through what is not working and set goals for achievement. Sometimes crucial conversations must be had. The tools of the 30-60-90-day plan, plus/delta, PDSA, data questions, and instructional strategies already in their areas of expertise equipped the ERS staff to build working relationships. Some of the ERS staff used data notebooks and questions (Cornett), others common formative assessments (Higgins), and others PDSAs (Crowe) as their go-to tools, but all use all tools.

As the conversation continued, the ERSs indicated they use the PLC as the means to review data and build common approach plans with teachers. In the beginning, those agendas are predetermined for the PLC, but teachers are empowered to take the reins as soon as they are ready. Other tools regularly used were the quarterly reports, Consensograms, and again in a quick choral answer, "data questions!"

Jim Hamm in a separate conversation would add the PDSA as *the* trust tool. He reflected, "One of my favorite quotes is from Steven Covey, 'Success can only move at the speed of trust.' Many people have trouble trusting anyone in a broken system. The PDSA process is the mechanism that bridges the trust gap. People begin to trust the process first and then the people leading the process. That is probably one of the most important parts of the work. After all, our work is with the people, not the process. They conduct and improve the process."

Some ERSs were responsible for building the mission, vision, values, review of the leadership assessment, and school data to determine the 30-60-90-day plan priorities. In other teams the ERL and principal led that process. In some schools staff leadership teams were very engaged from the beginning. As these education recovery staff shared their stories, no two were the same.

Crystal, Kim, and Debra briefly spoke as to how important it is that the ERS is not an evaluator but a coach. Going into classrooms requires building a human connection with the people with whom they are working to build a sense of "we are in this together."

Part III has been about tried and true strategies that worked for educators from the state level to the classroom level and back again. Does everybody have to do all of them to be successful? No, but leaders must have all of them in the toolkit to be successful.

Part IV will share case studies of how a high school in a small rural district with a central office without capacity became the first to exit priority status, how two rural districts with district-level and school-level issues built processes to be successful through persistence and support, how a large urban high school became the first of the priority schools in the largest district to exit priority status, and how the largest district with the most schools has taught the state about working effectively with them.

KEY IDEAS

- Quarterly reporting on progress is a must at the school and district levels.
- Making connections among all levels of the work with graphic organizers is worth the time (linkage charts, systems checks) to answer, "Where do I fit?"

- Common quality tools make work predictable and provide feedback (plus/delta).
- Teacher working conditions information is crucial to system improvement.
- Support for teachers and administrators must be just in time.
- Flexibility with scheduling of interventions is a must.
- Leaders and support must model behaviors they want to see.

Part IV

CASE STUDIES AND LESSONS LEARNED WITH CONTINUED CHALLENGES

We can do anything we want if we stick to it long enough.

—Helen Keller

Chapter 8

Case Studies

D180 has met with some successes in student achievement and building sustainable systems. D180 has had some significant challenges that are yet unresolved. Much of the Kentucky land area is rural with 55.72 percent of the population living in metropolitan areas, primarily the triangle that goes from Louisville to Cincinnati (Ohio) and back to Lexington, Kentucky (U.S. Census Bureau). The remainder of the population is scattered throughout the rest of the Commonwealth. Rural areas in D180 in general have been more successful in student achievement improvement overall than the urban schools.

Still, college and career readiness numbers are up in all priority schools. There are some effective systems in all priority schools but not all systems in all schools are where they need to be. The lessons learned through D180 speak to the idea that continuous improvement of systems focused on the data and information available if allowed to continue can and will produce effective and efficient systems.

Four case studies are shared here to assist educators and policy makers in further understanding how seemingly messy and even chaotic building systems can be. Many educators when asked would say they just want to teach or just want to be in the classroom with the children. America's schools must realize that the systems to deliver the ultimate learning experiences are as diverse as the students being served and as challenging as the educators who help create the experiences. The organizational structures must be flexible, focused, and effective. America's schools must be kaleidoscopes reflecting light by tweaking and viewing in different settings, but always beautiful as they develop.

CASE STUDY 1: A SMALL RURAL HIGH SCHOOL AND A DISTRICT WITHOUT CAPACITY TO SUPPORT IT

The District: Leslie County Schools
Priority School within the District: Leslie County High School Identified 2010 (Cohort 1)
Description of the School and District

"Leslie County High School is home to 540 students in grades 9-12. (10,000 residents in the county). This is the only high school in the county. It is the largest school in the district, serving students from diverse areas in the county. The area is a sparsely-populated, mountainous region. Many of the students travel approximately 30 miles over rugged terrain to reach the school.

Above all, poverty is an issue that overwhelms the community. The Kentucky Division of Nutrition and Health Services (2009) estimate that 69.25% of the student body at Leslie County High School receive free or reduced lunches. The most recent United States Census establishes that 30% of individuals in the county are in poverty and that only 40% of individuals are currently employed.

Most compelling is the fact that per capita income is only $11,674 compared to the national average of $21,587. Thus, individuals in the county receive nearly half of typical earnings when compared to others across Kentucky and the nation. Also, the disability rate of 33% is high compared to the national average of 19%. Another significant factor is that only 54% of residents 25 years and older have a high school diploma compared to the national average of 80%. 9% possess a Bachelor's degree or higher compared to the national average of 24%.

The low educational attainment of individuals indicates their detachment from the educational system and their previous negative experiences in schooling matters. It is reasonable to assume that due to their experiences, individuals in the county do not view the educational system as an impetus to successful life endeavors. Their children, in turn, may be affected by views regarding their high school experience.

The area is a depressed area where there is not an abundance of qualified job applicants as is proven by trends in past job postings and screening processes.

In previous years, many education jobs have even been filled by persons with emergency certification with no actual teaching or educational experiences." (Leslie County School District 2010, 2–6)

A visitor to Leslie County would learn quickly that it is the home of former University of Kentucky football standout and NFL player Tim Couch, the redbud capital of the world, and the location of the first speech given by Richard Nixon after his resignation when the Richard Nixon Center was dedicated in Hyden in July 1978.

Leslie County High School was one of the first ten priority schools identified. As soon as it was identified, an assessment was conducted. The assessment was based on nine state standards and eighty-eight performance indicators. This Kentucky document known as SISI had been developed for school improvement as a part of KERA and had been used in scholastic audits for several years. (Described in more detail in part III.)

To determine the capacity of the principal, school council, and district, the leadership assessment and later diagnostic review continues to be used in school improvement work. The chart in table 8.1 shows the deficiency findings for the district and the high school for the first two administrations of a leadership assessment in Leslie.

Reason for Being Notable

Leslie County High School was in the bottom ten indexed Kentucky high schools. It is in traditional coal country where jobs have declined. The school's math and language arts scores on state assessments had steadily declined. Leslie is unique and the subject of this case study due to the leadership determination from the leadership assessments. The principal who had been in place for almost a year and the council at the school were determined to have capacity. The district leadership was determined not to have capacity.

Leslie County High School would be the first in Kentucky to exit priority status of the original ten identified. Since exiting priority status, Leslie has consistently improved and maintained high rankings in the state accountability model. The approach at Leslie of the state education recovery team and the leadership in the district were critical components for their improvement.

Approach at the School

Several of the quality tools and strategies that were successful are discussed in part III of this book using Leslie County examples. Perhaps the key to Leslie County High School's continuous improvement approach for success is the determination of leadership from the beginning. As they wrote in their SIG application,

> Following the 2009-2010 Leadership Assessment Reports, Leslie County High School has formed a leadership team whose sole purpose has been to analyze the audit results and to plan methods for addressing each of the suggested growth areas (deficiencies). (Leslie County School District 2010, 7)

Table 8.1 Leadership Assessment Deficiencies Leslie County High School and District

District 2010 Leadership Assessment Deficiencies	High School 2010 Leadership Assessment Deficiencies	District 2012 Leadership Assessment Deficiencies	High School 2012 Leadership Assessment Deficiencies
Leslie County School District leadership did not act on the next steps or recommendations outlined in the October 2006 scholastic audit report.	The school council and principal have not developed or approved a comprehensive school improvement plan to guide the school toward increased student achievement.	The superintendent has not ensured administrative staff leadership skills match with appropriate jobs and responsibilities to lead all schools to meet the district 20x20 strategic plan goals.	The principal has not established procedures to ensure that all students have the tools they need to be successful in a competitive economy.
The superintendent has not adopted a no excuses approach to improving student achievement.	The school council and principal have not accepted responsibility in shared decision making as defined by state statute.	The superintendent and district leadership have not ensured that instructional and assessment practices are rigorous and challenge students to think at high levels.	The principal has not created an instructional culture for twenty-first-century learners.
The superintendent does not have a process to monitor the effectiveness of district programs and hold staff accountable for successful implementation.	The school council and principal do not ensure that the adopted instructional practices policy is fully implemented and technology is integrated in classroom instruction.	The superintendent has not ensured that school-based instructional technology resources are effectively utilized by teachers and students to enhance instruction and improve student achievement.	The principal does not ensure that all teachers are using rigorous instructional strategies to implement the curriculum.

District 2010 Leadership Assessment Deficiencies	High School 2010 Leadership Assessment Deficiencies	District 2012 Leadership Assessment Deficiencies	High School 2012 Leadership Assessment Deficiencies
District leadership has not developed a comprehensive communications plan.	The principal does not ensure that classroom assessments are frequent, rigorous, and authentic	The superintendent has not ensured that all schools provide equitable opportunities for a comprehensive instructional program.	The principal has not cultivated all staff members to successfully function independently and be self-directing.
District leadership does not clearly communicate expectations for developing a fully aligned curriculum, designing, and administering rigorous assessments, and delivering differentiated instructional strategies to high school leadership and staff.	The principal does not lead the staff in ongoing data analysis to determine the school's instructional and organizational effectiveness.	The superintendent has not ensured that discussions occur among grade levels and between schools (elementary to middle and middle to high school) to vertically align the curriculum.	The school council has not fulfilled its role and responsibility to serve as the governing body for Leslie County High School.
District leadership has not provided a strategic comprehensive district improvement plan that will lead the high school to proficiency.	A student-centered culture that is focused on student needs and academic achievement has not been created.		All stakeholder groups are not involved in the educational process.

District 2010 Leadership Assessment Deficiencies	High School 2010 Leadership Assessment Deficiencies	District 2012 Leadership Assessment Deficiencies	High School 2012 Leadership Assessment Deficiencies
Determination: The district leadership assessment team has determined that the district does not have the capability and capacity to manage the intervention in Leslie County High School.	Determination: School Council Authority: The school leadership assessment team has determined that the school council has the capability and capacity to continue its roles and responsibilities established in KRS 160.345. Principal Authority: The school leadership assessment team has determined that the principal has the capability and capacity to continue his roles and responsibilities established in KRS 160.345. (Pending approval from the USDOE the principal of Leslie County High School may remain in this position for the 2010–11 school year. However, after one year of implementing the intervention plan, if Leslie County High School has not made sufficient progress toward the annual goals and implementation of the intervention plan, the *principal shall be removed.*)	Determination: District leadership does have the ability to manage the intervention of Leslie County High School	Determination: Council Authority: The school council does have the ability to lead the intervention and does have the capability and capacity to continue its roles and responsibilities established in KRS 160.345. Principal Authority: The principal does have the ability to lead the intervention and should remain as principal of the school to continue his roles and responsibilities established in KRS 160.345.

Using the 30-60-90-day big rock planning tool, this team was composed of the sometimes two-member and sometimes three-member education recovery staff (always an ERL and at least one ERS), the principal, the assistant principal, both guidance counselors, the school instructional technology person, and teacher leaders as appropriate. The leadership team drove improvements at the school.

The original three big rocks were school culture vision, academic performance, and data-based decision making. Action plans were built and monitored on thirty-day goals with reviews at least weekly by the leadership team. Everyone focused and modeled expectations (the 30-60-90-day plan is in appendix B). The principal engaged students directly by asking their opinions of what good instruction looked like and shared the outcomes with teachers who had completed the same activity.

Conversations about what was expected of students to get Leslie County High School out of this state designation were a regular occurrence with students. Perhaps one of the most telling examples of the effectiveness of such an approach was one day in probably year three of Leslie County's improvement when a young man was being carted off by local authorities to answer for a violation of law. He asked if he could speak to the assistant principal before he left because he wanted to know when his scores on a key benchmark assessment were going to be back!

The rural challenge of having highly qualified staff to ensure students are exposed to higher levels of learning exists in Leslie. The leadership team with the education recovery staff and school administrative staff determined how to match up the student needs with the skills of the teachers and then how to equip the teachers who needed additional skills.

The flexibility and agility of staffing and coaching of staff has been and is crucial for improvement. Yes, they had to purchase some technology software and programs to supplement where teacher skills were not available. But teachers learned those technologies as well to see what students could learn through them and thus used them more effectively.

The deficiencies noted in 2012 indicated a higher level of instruction rather than being sure compliant basics were in place. In the full-length report, significant improvement from the first to second leadership assessments had occurred in all areas regarding staffing and building capacity of instruction as well as planning for building capacity and job-embedded support.

Teacher evaluation and determination of effectiveness was also tied within the school to goals set for student performance. As a result, student performance continuously improved. At their second leadership assessment, Leslie High School had many areas of level 3 performance around comprehensive planning, personnel evaluation and support, long-term planning, professional growth needs, connections to student data, building capacity, and job-embedded staff development. They received a level 4 (top ranking) for staff assignment processes.

Approach at the District

Superintendent Larry Sparks shared that it felt like he had been "punched in the gut" when the team from the Kentucky Department of Education delivered the 2010 leadership assessment. When he and his school board chair met with the education recovery director for the east, she told them that she understood but the fact was they would have another assessment in less than two years and the deficiencies would have to be corrected.

The district not having capacity meant that the Kentucky commissioner of education/designee would ensure that the district regained capacity. There was no precedent for this exact relationship. After all, the school and council had capacity. Both the board chair and Superintendent Sparks were open to whatever support came their way.

It was determined that the education recovery director (ERD) would meet with central office staff for training every two weeks for the first three months. After that the ERD would meet with Mr. Sparks weekly after she met with the leadership team at Leslie County High School.

And so it began. The biweekly training was loosely based on the seven Baldrige categories for performance excellence with each position developing a linkage chart (explained in part III) to connect with Leslie County High School processes. The ERL from the school was a part of these sessions so that she would know what was happening with the model. The group then began to develop a strategic plan for the district as well as support for the high school.

It was rocky. Reinforcements had to be brought in from the Kentucky Department of Education to review special education processes. Other consultants with specific Kentucky law and regulation knowledge were called in to assist the rookie-to-Kentucky ERD. The cooperation from KDE was free-flowing and crucial for building leadership capacity at the district office.

One of the first concrete plans that came from the district training was a communications plan for the district. They determined all the ways communication happened in and through the district and how that communication flowed. Then they consulted parents and community members to find out how people wanted communication to happen. The plan that resulted has been used by other Kentucky districts as a model. By the time the second leadership assessment came around, the district had improved measures from level 1 to level 3 out of a possible 4 in several key areas. Most importantly those areas were comprehensive and effective planning, school organization, and resources and leadership. They received a level 4 in vision and the collaborative process. The district was determined to have capacity.

CASE STUDY 2: TWO SMALL RURAL DISTRICTS WITH RESTARTS

Districts: Fleming County Schools (Eastern Kentucky) and Caverna Independent School District (Western Kentucky)

Priority School within the District: Fleming County High School and Caverna High School

Description of the Districts

Fleming County is located geographically in northeastern Kentucky. According to the U.S. Census Bureau in 2016 the county had a population of 14,507 people of whom 25 percent were school-age. With a racial composition of 96 percent white, 2 percent African American, and the remaining 2 percent Asian and multiracial, 57 percent of those aged sixteen and over are in the workforce, primarily in farming. There is a 20 percent poverty rate with a per capita income of $21,600. Data USA indicates that the economy is mixed among administrative, production, and management positions with approximately 5 percent in farming and food production. The county seat is Flemingsburg. The land area is 348.54 square miles. Fleming has been designated the Covered Bridge Capital of Kentucky. The school district serves 2,286 students in grades K–12.

Caverna Independent School District (CISD) is an independent district crossing between Hart and Barren Counties in Kentucky. Geographically CISD sits in an area of 22.48 square miles in central Kentucky and slightly to the southwest. CISD service area has a population of 5,881 with approximately 25 percent of them of school age. The poverty rate is 28 percent with most workers being employees in production or transportation. The population is 88 percent Caucasian with 9 percent African American, 1 percent Native American, and the remaining 2 percent composed of Asian and multiracial individuals. Cave City and Horse Cave are the towns in the school district.

Mammoth Cave is a major tourist attraction in the area. Average household income in Cave City was $29,821 in 2015. The district serves 693 students in grades K–12 (U.S. Census 2016).

Reason for Being Notable

Both districts are rural and relatively small. They both have identified priority schools in them. Caverna High School was identified in cohort 1 of the

Table 8.2 Fleming Leadership Assessment/Diagnostic Review Deficiencies

District 2012 Leadership Assessment Deficiencies	District 2014 Diagnostic Review Deficiencies Addendum
There is a lack of clarity in the understanding of roles and responsibilities among central office staff.	There is little or no evidence of improvement about this deficiency.
The school district and community do not have a shared understanding of the characteristics of high-performing schools.	There is little or no evidence of improvement about this deficiency.
The high school is not focused on high academic achievement for all students.	There is little or no evidence of improvement about this deficiency.
Instructional practice in the high school is not of sufficient rigor to create high academic achievement.	There is little or no evidence of improvement about this deficiency.
The classroom assessments at the high school are not consistently rigorous, authentic, or aligned with current academic standards.	There is little or no evidence of improvement about this deficiency.
Teachers at the high school do not routinely collaborate in a common protocol to analyze student work for informing instruction.	This deficiency has been partially addressed.
	The diagnostic review identified eighteen improvement priorities to address for the 2015 review.
District Authority: District leadership does not have the ability to manage the intervention of Fleming County High School.	**District Authority: District leadership does not have the ability to manage the intervention of Fleming County High School.**

SIG process and Fleming High School was identified in cohort 3 of the SIG process. At the same time the schools had a leadership assessment/diagnostic review because they had been identified as priority, the district also had a review. With the first review Caverna district was determined to have capacity and Fleming district was determined not to have capacity to support the turnaround in two review cycles. At the second review for Caverna the district was determined not to have capacity.

In both cases factors external to the SIG process and authorizing regulations were identified through the review process. In both cases the leadership assessment/diagnostic process information triggered another Kentucky statute for state assistance or management. With the application of the state statute KRS 158.785 Fleming and Caverna became state assisted. They are models of how existing legislation/processes and aligned interventions can assist in systemic, sustainable change.

In both cases superintendents were nonrenewed or resigned/retired while interventions continued based on the findings of the reviews. As of the winter of 2017 both Caverna and Fleming have exited state assistance. Student performance continues to improve with the help of aligned processes at the district level.

It is important to note that the AdvancED diagnostic review process does not include a capacity determination. The Kentucky Department of Education school improvement processes include a determination based on the AdvancED review. It is conducted at the end of the diagnostic review visit with the team by a KDE-trained staff member. The recommendation is then given to the commissioner of education for review as required by statute for final determination.(KRS 160.346)

Approach at the District in Fleming

The political ramifications of receiving a lack of capacity designation from the state differ with each district. Fleming is a study in establishing urgency for improvement. Between 2012 and 2015 there were three different superintendents. In December 2013 the Kentucky Board of Education voted to place Fleming under state assistance due to the results of a management audit triggered by financial and budgetary concerns.

In assistance the district received guidance from Jim Hamm, who coordinated the support from KDE for district work to address process issues. An additional diagnostic review in 2015 indicated for a third time that the district did not have capacity to support turnaround. The superintendent retired. The third superintendent was hired from out of state knowing the district was in state assistance. He also had the results of the 2014 leadership assessment/

diagnostic review with eighteen priorities for improvement. He was also facing a 2015 review.

New superintendent Dr. Brian Creasman and the Fleming County Board of Education established a vision for Fleming to become a District of Distinction in the Kentucky Accountability System. And this happened.

- In the 2015–16 school year Fleming County Schools were distinguished.
- By the diagnostic review in March 2017 the eighteen improvement priorities were reduced to three. The district gained capacity!
- Fleming was cited in the report for a powerful practice for its own internal review/monitoring process.
- In the spring of 2017 Fleming exited state assistance.

Is student performance where they want it to be? No, but continuous improvement is moving them forward. AdvancED thought well enough of the progress of the use of the diagnostic review by Fleming that they wrote a case study, "A District Moves from Turnaround to Transformation in Rural Kentucky. Fleming County 2013–2016."

Approach at the District in Caverna

The district was initially determined to have capacity to support the high school. Perhaps surprisingly, as small a district as Caverna is, the financial sustainability has been consistently strong. The acceptance of the three-person education recovery team for improvement at the high school and the understanding of the team's role by all impacted by the team's presence was slow. Caverna already had strengths in acceptance from the community and the climate in general.

The Caverna district had a very small district office where personnel were concerned. Resource functions were controlled from the central office and alignment with 30-60-90-day planning was difficult. The education recovery director for the west worked with the central office but found it difficult to break the barriers necessary for alignment and success for the interventions that education recovery provided in the early days of implementation.

With the 2012 leadership assessment it was clear that barriers to sustainability planning and meeting the requirements of the SIG grant were present. The district was determined with the second review not to have capacity.

Still, the education recovery team continued to work daily at the high school and provided the required quarterly reports to the education recovery director in the west who reported them to the commissioner of education.

Table 8.3 Caverna Leadership Assessment/Diagnostic Review Deficiencies

District 2010 Leadership Assessment Deficiencies	District 2012 Leadership Assessment Deficiencies	District 2014 Diagnostic Review Deficiencies Addendum
District leadership has not facilitated effective comprehensive district and school improvement planning to drive necessary changes in teaching and learning to sustain continuous improvement.	The superintendent has not established a professional culture.	This deficiency has been partially addressed.
District leadership has not systematically monitored student achievement, instructional programs, and services to ensure improved student and school performance.	The superintendent has not established professional relationships with all district and high school employees.	There is little or no evidence of improvement about this deficiency.
District leadership has not ensured that instruction is consistently rigorous, standards-based, and differentiated to meet the unique learning needs of Caverna's diverse student population.	The superintendent has not developed or articulated a formal plan to sustain academic progress at the high school beyond the school improvement grant phase.	There is little or no evidence of improvement about this deficiency.
District leadership has not provided an aligned curriculum document for the Caverna school district.	The superintendent seldom evaluates the extent to which allocated resources (that is, human, fiscal, and physical) are producing the desired impact.	There is little or no evidence of improvement about this deficiency.
	The superintendent has not maximized the evaluation process to foster leadership capacity.	There is little or no evidence of improvement about this deficiency.
Strengths were noted in culture, communication, community support, and record keeping.	Strengths were noted as in 2010 with addition of evaluation process and professional development for capacity building.	Diagnostic review identified seventeen improvement priorities to be addressed before the 2016–17 reviews.
District Authority 2010: District leadership has the capability and capacity to manage the intervention at Caverna High School.	District Authority 2012: District leadership does not have the ability to manage the intervention of Caverna High School.	District Authority 2014: District leadership does not have the ability to manage the intervention of Caverna High School.

Some progress was made across that time in professional learning particularly, but all systems had not been built based on the education recovery model and tools.

In June 2014 the twenty-seven-year superintendent veteran retired. Cornelius Faulkner, who had held several positions in the district, was chosen as superintendent beginning in the 2014–15 school year. A management audit (KRS 160.346.) was conducted in the summer/fall of 2014 to ensure the systems were in place for Caverna to be successful. The audit recommended state assistance, which was agreed to by the new superintendent and the school board.

Jim Hamm was appointed as the assistance coach. One of the advantages of state assistance and management is that the coach or manager assigned to the district can help ensure that the assistance coming from KDE is aligned and helpful. It is not unusual for different departments to have different activities going on in low-performing districts. Assistance or management makes sure that those supports align and that different departments at KDE who may be aiding are not doubly requiring things. Alignment of the help is crucial. PDSAs help.

Superintendent Faulkner with his leadership team by the 2016–17 diagnostic review had satisfactorily addressed six of the seventeen improvement priorities and partially addressed the other eleven. There were processes in place that were transparent for curriculum development and use of data as well as the monitoring of instruction. One of the positives noted in the conclusion of the diagnostic review was that the school board had become actively engaged in understanding and hearing reports on student performance and aligned support actions.

Determination: District leadership does have the capacity to implement and manage the three improvement priorities developed from the diagnostic review (February 26–March 1, 2017). In June 2017, the Kentucky Board of Education released Caverna Independent from state assistance.

Conclusions from Two Small Rural Districts for Sustainability

The entire leadership assessments and diagnostic review reports, SIG applications, and reviews can be located on the Kentucky Department of Education website. The reports provide performance data. District reports can also be accessed there too. All the documents inform improvement processes.

If the only concerns are math, literacy, ACT scores, and college and career readiness, the data show struggling but moving forward with continuous improvement. Some of the improvement is staggering in a good way! What is most telling is that even without the most favorable of conditions, ready acceptance of interventions, or retention of the same people in the positions over a long period of time, systems can survive and get better with the persistence of the coaches of empowering the people to make the necessary changes based on the use of common processes and tools.

KDE education recovery staff was not steadily the same in these settings across the years. For Fleming, there would be three education recovery directors in the east. For Caverna there would be three also in the west. School ER staff would have turnover. And yet with focused attention by the Kentucky Board of Education (for schools in assistance and management) with regular reporting and questioning supportive feedback, the work continues moving forward.

CASE STUDY 3: A LARGE URBAN TRADITIONAL HIGH SCHOOL

The District: Jefferson County Schools (Louisville)
Priority School within in the District: Fern Creek Traditional High School Identified 2010 (Cohort 1)
Description of the School and District (From the 2009–10 SIG Application)
Fern Creek (FCTHS) was a Non–Title I school. For 2009, Fern Creek met nine out of thirteen (69.2 percent) of its NCLB target goals. Fern Creek did meet their NCLB annual measurable objectives for all student groups in reading. Fern Creek did not meet their NCLB annual measurable objectives for the following student groups in mathematics: all students, white, African American, and free/reduced lunch.

Fern Creek High School is one of twenty-one high schools in JCPS, with an enrollment of 1,470 in 2010. Not only was the school facing years of low test scores and the stigma of not meeting NCLB's adequate yearly progress (AYP) since 2004, the district student assignment plan segregated poor minority students rather than spreading diversity across the district. The student assignment plan divided the district into three networks. Each network contained high schools labeled as a district magnet school and other high schools labeled by professional career themes.

Students living in all three networks could apply to attend one of the district magnet schools regardless of where they lived. This process was an attempt to provide access to the various magnets and programs throughout the district. However, the resulting reality or the process was that students who were higher achieving and from higher socioeconomic backgrounds in the district applied and were accepted to the district magnet schools because they had good grades, high achievement scores, and few if any discipline problems.

Table 8.4 Fern Creek Traditional High School Leadership Assessment Deficiencies

High School Deficiencies 2010 Leadership Assessment	High School Deficiencies 2012 Leadership Assessment
The principal and council do not focus on delivery of the curriculum, instruction, and assessment to meet students' needs.	The principal has not ensured all teachers use rigorous instructional and assessment practices that require higher-order thinking skills.
The principal and school council do not adequately address the learning deficiencies of struggling students in reading and math.	The principal has not ensured all teachers utilize opportunities to enhance and expand instruction through student use of technology.
The principal and school council do not create a plan that targets learning gaps and supports structures necessary for high student achievement.	The principal has not provided necessary supports and resources to the Freshman Academy to ensure the academic and behavioral success of students.
The principal and the school council do not fully implement a school governance structure as mandated by state statute.	The principal and assistant principals do not consistently use the Teacher Evaluation Plan to address individual teachers' growth needs.
The principal and school council do not focus on the critical learning needs of gifted nor struggling students.	
The principal and school council do not provide guidance in recognizing and addressing cultural and socioeconomic differences of the school's diverse populations.	
Determination:	Determination:
School Council Authority: The school leadership assessment team has determined that the council does not have sufficient capacity to manage the recovery of the school and recommends the council's authority be transferred to the superintendent.	School council is in advisory role and authority was not determined. Principal Authority: The principal does have the ability to lead the intervention and should remain as principal of the school to continue his roles and responsibilities established in KRS 160.345.
Principal Authority: The school leadership assessment team has determined that the principal does not have the capability and capacity to continue the roles and responsibilities established in KRS 160.345.	
This finding was appealed to the commissioner of education and the principal remained in his role.	

The assignment plan resulted in FCTHS having a distinct disadvantage in terms of recruiting students into the school. Approximately 1,700 students living in the residence area of FCTHS are enrolled in other schools. The average median income of the Fern Creek zip code, 40291, was $62,575 in 2010. Only 10.6 percent of students attending FCTHS who lived in the 40291 zip code had a household median income of $62,575 or higher; most students were attending other schools in the district (Jefferson County Public Schools 2011).

The enrollment process impacted the makeup of the student body at FCTHS because it allowed students in the residence area the option of applying to district magnet programs rather than attending their home school.

The school had a culture that was influenced by the local teacher association. Members of the turnaround team (visiting school leadership assessment team 2009) noted that the school had a teacher-centered culture rather than a student-centered culture. The teacher contract required teachers to have fifty minutes of planning each day and could only be required to stay after school sixty minutes each week. In the opinion of the visiting team these restrictions contributed to a culture that did not focus on addressing student needs. Such a school culture built around teacher requirements was an additional barrier for this priority school to increasing student achievement.

The teachers also seemed to lack ownership of the curriculum due to the district process of providing a prepackaged curriculum, pacing guide, and assessments based on the standards. Although this method perhaps saved time, the standards not being deconstructed by the teachers left out an important step that ensures that the teachers understand the curriculum themselves before teaching it. Therefore, many teachers did not own the content or have a clear understanding of how the activities provided tied to the standards.

As soon as the schools were identified, the leadership assessment was conducted. As in the other case studies in part IV, the assessment was based on nine state standards and eighty-eight performance indicators to determine the capacity of the principal, school council, and district. The chart in table 8.4 shows the deficiency findings for the school for the first two administrations of the leadership assessment.

Reason for Being Notable

Fern Creek Traditional High School was one of the first ten schools identified as a priority school in Kentucky, one of six in Jefferson County. FCTHS personnel chose the restaffing model. The entire faculty had to be screened by the principal and 50 percent of the faculty had to be removed before the start of the 2010–11 school year. In August 2010, Fern Creek began the school year with thirty-eight new teachers to the building of which eighteen were first-year teachers in a total staff of seventy-six teachers.

During the early days of the turnaround process the principal and the leadership had to make some tough choices that sometimes put them on the opposite side of the district's protocols and procedures. The leadership team stayed the course and the school exited priority status in 2015. The school has scored proficient on the past two state assessments. Here is what happened.

The school's enrollment has increased by approximately four hundred students since 2010, has the lowest teacher turnover of any PLA school in the district, and is now identified for funding as a Title I school. The college and career readiness rate for graduating seniors has increased from 19 percent in 2010 to 91 percent in 2016. Only one administrator from the original leadership team is no longer at the school.

Approach at the School

Many of the quality tools and strategies mentioned in part III of this book have been successful and sustainable at Fern Creek High School. As the turnaround process began the school leadership team and the educational recovery staff used the 2009–10 leadership assessment to determine the three big rocks that would drive the school improvement process and 30-60-90-day planning. The team identified the following as big rocks: implementing PLCs, data/targeted interventions, and improving customer service. After the big rocks had been identified, 30-60-90-day implementation plans were developed.

The turnaround team designed a systematic approach to implement PLCs school-wide to work with English II and Algebra II teachers to analyze individual student data using this analysis to make instructional changes. Common assessments were designed first with each question being tied to a specific standard. Data days were implemented giving teachers time to look at assessment results. During a data day, teachers examined assessment results and determined which standards their students had mastered and which they had not.

The standards-based approach to teaching and assessing allowed teachers to understand what their students knew and did not know. The second part of the data day gave teachers time to design individual intervention systems to help meet individual student needs. FCTHS developed a red, yellow, and green intervention system giving individual interventions based on how the student scored on the assessment.

By implementing a systematic approach to monitor student data, instructional adjustments were made and interventions were designed. As a part of this intentional implementation, there was a change in the academic culture at FCTHS. The development of the monitoring student data process was a collaborative effort between the ER staff, administration, and teachers. Once Algebra II and English II teachers embedded the student monitoring process, the ER staff began to share this process with other departments.

English II and Algebra II teachers modeled the process with teachers in other content areas. By the beginning of the second year of turnaround, this systematic approach of monitoring student progress was implemented into all departments.

Effective PLCs eventually became a way of life at Fern Creek and the venue to analyze data while making instructional changes. Fern Creek recently received the DuFour Award, a $25,000 award named in honor of Rick DuFour that recognizes one outstanding PLC demonstrating exceptional levels of student achievement. Their turnaround journey has led the school to become a national model for professional learning communities.

CASE STUDY 4: THE LARGEST DISTRICT IN THE STATE WITH THE MOST PRIORITY SCHOOLS

The District: Jefferson County Schools
  Priority Schools within in the District:
  Cohort 1: 2009–10 Identified: Fern Creek Traditional High School (has exited status), Frost Middle School (has restructured), The Academy @ Shawnee, Valley Traditional High School (has exited status), Western High School, and Western Middle School
  Cohort 2: 2010–11 Identified: Doss Middle School, Fairdale High School, Iroquois High School, Knight Middle School, Seneca High School, Southern High School, and Waggener Traditional High Academy (has exited status)
  Cohort 3: 2011–12 Identification: Frederick Law Olmstead Academy, Myers Middle (has closed), Stuart Middle (has restructured), Thomas Jefferson Middle, and Westport Middle
  Cohort 4: 2015–16 Identified: Byck Elementary, Moore Elementary, and Roosevelt Perry Elementary
  Cohort 5: 2016–17 Identified: Maupin Elementary and Wellington Elementary
  Description of Jefferson County
Jefferson County is in the northwest central region of Kentucky on the border with Indiana. The largest city in Jefferson County is Louisville, which is also the largest city in the Commonwealth of Kentucky. Within Jefferson County are eighty-three incorporated taxing jurisdictions. Jefferson County had a population in 2016 of 765,352 people. The ethnic composition of the

county is 72.7 percent white, 21.8 percent African American, and 5 percent Hispanic, with below 1 percent of Asian and Native Americans.

Sixty-six percent of the population is in the labor force. Per capita income is $28,822 and the poverty rate is 15.4 percent (U.S. Bureau of Labor Statistics 2016). Seventy-four percent of employment is in private wage/salary positions, 5 percent government, and 21 percent self-employed (City-Data n.d.).

Covering 380 square miles, Jefferson County is home to Churchill Downs, the Louisville Slugger Museum, the Muhammad Ali Center, and the Waterfront Park. Louisville is home base for GE Appliances, Humana, Yum! Brands (Kentucky Fried Chicken, Papa John's, etc.), UPS Airlines, and Texas Road House, among others. There are thirteen colleges and universities located in Jefferson County with the University of Louisville among the most recognizable nationwide in the group.

Louisville is home to a Baptist and a Presbyterian theological seminary. There are ninety-nine private schools serving approximately 32,000 students (Private School Review n.d.). Seventy-eight percent of the private schools are sponsored by the Catholic Diocese. The Kentucky School for the Blind is in the county. Anchorage Independent School District is located geographically in Jefferson County serving 363 students.

According to the Jefferson County school report card on the Kentucky Department of Education website, the school district serves 96,581 students in a growing population. The ethnic composition of the school system does not reflect by proportion the composition of the county. Of the students 46.6 percent are white, 36.1 percent are African American, 9.6 percent are Hispanic, 3.8 percent are Asian, less than 1 percent are American Indian or Native Hawaiian, and 3.8 percent are multiracial. The poverty rate measured by free and reduced lunch eligibility is 60 percent.

There are 173 schools in the Jefferson County Public Schools. On the Kentucky report card in 2016 the accountability designation for Jefferson County public schools was needs improvement. Within the district are some of both the highest and lowest academically performing schools in the Commonwealth. There are 6,071 teachers, 82 percent of whom have advanced degrees. The Jefferson County Teachers Association has been the recognized bargaining agent for certified personnel since 1968.

Reason for Being Notable

Along with being the most populated school district in the state, Jefferson County public schools receive attention from media and public interest sources daily as the district attempts to serve the academic, social, and behavioral needs of its population.

Table 8.5 Jefferson County Schools District Leadership Assessment/Diagnostic Review Deficiencies

District Leadership Assessment 2009–10 Deficiencies	District Diagnostic Review 2016
District and school leadership in persistently low-achieving schools has failed to establish a culture of high expectations and academic rigor for all students.	Implement and monitor an "instructional process" in all priority schools that ensures teachers 1) inform students of learning expectations and standards of performance, 2) use exemplars to further inform students of learning expectations, 3) use formative assessments to guide continual modifications of curriculum and instruction, and 4) provide students with timely and specific feedback about their learning.
District staffing patterns have not ensured that proficient and highly competent teachers and administrators are placed and retained in persistently low-achieving schools.	Improve student engagement in learning by identifying and implementing with fidelity research aligned instructional strategies such as 1) student collaboration, 2) development of critical/higher order thinking skills, 3) use of personalization/individualization strategies, and 4) use of technology as instructional tools and resources. Provide professional learning opportunities, ongoing support for teachers such as coaching, and effective monitoring processes to systematically implement instructional approaches that authentically engage students in their learning resulting in improved student achievement and success.
High teacher turnover rates in persistently low-achieving schools significantly reduces the ability to build school-wide instructional capacity.	
The superintendent has not ensured that fiscal and human resources allocated to the persistently low-achieving schools are fully evaluated to determine impact on student achievement.	Create and implement an effective process that is consistently implemented by system and school leaders to formally and consistently monitor, support, and evaluate teachers in the use of instructional practices focused on higher levels of student success and achievement. These practices should include 1) teaching the approved curriculum, 2) use of appropriate and content-specific standards of professional practice, and 3) alignment of practices with the system's beliefs and values about teaching and learning.

District Leadership Assessment 2009–10 Deficiencies	District Diagnostic Review 2016
The district improvement plan does not include specific and measurable goals, objectives, and activities to improve student achievement, especially in reading and math.	Develop, implement, and monitor the impact of a consistent, well-defined, and ongoing process among all priority schools for collecting, analyzing, and using multiple assessments of student learning as well as data from an examination of professional practice (PGES). Use the data gathered from these sources to monitor and adjust curriculum, instruction, and assessment at the school level and guide a process of continuous improvement that results in verifiable improvement in student achievement.
Two exemplary strengths noted in the report: The planning process involves collecting, managing, and analyzing data and organizational effectiveness. Strengths and limitations are identified. Thirteen other standards were fully functional with an operational level of development and implementation.	Strengths noted were in 1) strategic vision/planning, 2) district restructure to include director of priority schools and education recovery director reporting weekly to superintendent's cabinet, 3) improved relationships with external partners including JCTA and legislators, 4) development of internal classroom assessment system, and 5) commitment to PLCs.
District Authority: The district leadership assessment team has determined that the district has the capability and capacity to manage the interventions in the district's six persistently low-achieving schools (Fern Creek Traditional High School, Robert Frost Middle School, Shawnee High School, Valley Traditional High School, Western MST Magnet High School, and Western Middle School).	**District Authority: District leadership does have the ability to manage the intervention of Jefferson County's nine priority schools reviewed, in addition to the other nine priority schools in the district. District leadership should incorporate the improvement priorities into the comprehensive district improvement plan. A monitoring system should be created to ensure that the district is implementing the district improvement plan with fidelity to meet the needs of all Jefferson County students.** **Specific attention must be focused on developing a culture of differentiated support and accountability for all district schools, but especially the priority schools. This includes a sharp focus in addressing the achievement gap, boosting professional learning effectiveness, and continuing to clarify systems within the district to support that work.**

Many reviews for improvement from private industry to national academic scholars as well as creative partnerships with local universities to improve performance have met with mixed success. Crime, violence, drug, and gang issues that exist in the city impact the work of JCPS daily as in most every urban area in the United States. The political discourse engages private and public voices.

If JCPS can address the academic barriers standing in the way of student success, then Kentucky is set on a course for consistent, continuous improvement for the future. JCPS is culturally diverse. If JCPS can address the social barriers that stand in the way of student success, then Kentucky is set on a course for consistent, continuous improvement for the future. If JCPS can close gaps with students, then Kentucky is set on a course for consistent, continuous improvement for the future. If JCPS does not build continuous improvement systems that are sustainable, then the goals of Kentucky education will not be met.

JCPS has much moving in the right direction. The struggle with the twenty-four identified priority schools in Jefferson County Schools is real. But if JCPS with the assistance of a continuous improvement approach can address the barriers to student success in these schools, then JCPS and Kentucky are set on a course for consistent, continuous improvement for the future. There is hope.

Fern Creek High School (subject of case study 3 of part IV) is in JCPS. There are two other JCPS schools that have exited priority status. The district and how it communicates and operates holds major keys to unlocking the rest of the barrier doors.

Approach at the District in Jefferson County Public Schools for Priority School Work

In JCPS six out of 173 schools were identified as priority in 2009–10. In the four other schools of the ten schools in cohort 1 no district had more than one school, and the priority school was the only high school in each of those districts. To begin with, JCPS would have to have a different approach to the same education recovery model (Kentucky Department of Education 2010).

In small districts, even where there was resistance to state intervention through education recovery, the process was an ERD and the superintendent with perhaps another central office person or two and a school board member began to see the plan for education recovery systems very quickly. Very few people made most of the decisions. In the smaller districts determining the root cause of low performance and identifying the big rocks was relatively simple as most had not used data to make decisions, most were struggling with new standards, and most had common cultural issues. All cohort 1 schools outside of Jefferson County had chosen the transformation model.

Jefferson would be and is different for education recovery and the D180 concept. With the first cohort of priority schools, the eighteen ERLs and ERSs (three per school) were hired as all other ER staff in the state were hired. They were on a memorandum of agreement with their home districts and the state to serve in Jefferson. (Ironically, cohort 1 year one would be the only time there has been a fully staffed priority school since the model began in Jefferson.)

There was one education recovery director for the district to provide support for the six schools. Across the first three cohorts twenty-two priority schools would be identified in Jefferson. The most schools in any other district was two. In addition, in cohort 3 the ERD for Jefferson picked up Trimble County High School in priority status to support.

Jefferson had a superintendent who had been in place since 2007 and had an organizational structure that included divisions of people to address data management, curriculum and instruction, professional development, human resources, finance, communications, academic services, operations services, and administration. Already in place were procedures for how to do things in Jefferson County public schools.

Student assignment had been and is a massive responsibility with court-ordered busing and subsequent court rulings addressing various issues about student assignment since 1975. In addition, the Jefferson County Teachers Association already had a contract in place addressing six thousand certified employees. How would that contract be interpreted and applied as the restaffing model was chosen by the six cohort 1 schools?

Restaffing meant the principal and at least 50 percent of the staff would be new to each of the settings unless the current principal had been determined to have capacity to lead the turnaround.

How would requirements for priority schools like 30-60-90-day planning and quarterly reporting be handled? Because data was collected at the district level, how would schools access what they needed? Would it be possible to produce a school-level report quarterly on the state's time frame? Who would monitor the SIG at the district level? The university partnership was with the University of Louisville already having a presence with working with individual schools and programs in some of the identified schools. What was happening already and how could the services of U of L assist in D180 work?

There were other large financial grants operating in the district. How would the work of those grants align with the work in the six identified schools? What professional development was already planned in JCPS for the schools involved? From where would the education recovery staff come? How would they understand and learn what they were to do in priority schools or apply the learnings from the two weeks of training in Louisville that first summer? How could it all come together as quickly as necessary? Most importantly, how could the six schools know that the district would take the priority process seriously and address the deficiencies at the district level with full district support for the initiative?

The ERD who was assigned to JCPS was Tom Price. Each of the three ERDs in Kentucky were to approach the work through the eyes of the SIGs the schools had written and apply the D180 model by coordinating and connecting with the universities and the central office. The relationship between the Kentucky Department of Education and Jefferson County public schools had been strained at times among various departments.

ERD Price had his work cut out for him, as did the education recovery teams assigned to the schools. There was a district office person who had been assigned to learn about D180 and who had attended the two-week training in Louisville. ERD Price spent much of his time in making connections in the 2010–11 school year. The six schools led by the ERL assigned to each were to follow the approved SIG plan. They would have quarterly reports. They would have 30-60-90-day plans.

Beyond that, how the teams worked, how they were accepted by leadership in each of the six schools, and how the day-to-day operations took place was a daily learning experience for the schools and ER teams. Very quickly there was evidence that some protocols, procedures, and contract negotiated stipulations did not align with what the SIG process and education recovery was to do.

Most notably in the restaffing model chosen by the six schools there would be the need to hire experienced teachers or those who had a specialty needed by the populations of students attending the priority schools. JCPS had a requirement that all first hires had to come from an overstaffing list, which was composed of JCPS employees who had been displaced from other schools. The six priority schools were then competing for the same people who may or may not have the expertise needed in the priority setting.

Another looming issue was that in many priority schools an intervention period was developed requiring every staff member to provide support in reading or math for a period each day or several times a week. One of the stipulations of the teacher contract was that teachers were to have no more than two preparations. Was this period considered a third? A third major issue was the role of ER staff as embedded professional developers.

The teacher contract had specific stipulations regarding the amount of a teacher's time that could be required outside of the school day for professional development as well as use of planning periods. The district also had district learning initiatives with required trainings. So who does what first? Much of ERD Price's time was spent in understanding the processes and

procedures and then sharing those in regular meetings with the education recovery leaders from the six schools.

At the district level that first year there were meetings with the district contact and later in the year with principals. These were beginning relationships
anticipating more schools being identified in year two. There was not an official monitoring process outside of the schools of the 30-60-90-day plans,
but it guided the ER staff work. Quarterly reports were a struggle the first
year as they began to be understood by the ER teams to help the schools. In
addition, the district centralized data. Access was a problem. The idea behind
data-driven decision making was that the school was to have ownership of the
report. That would take some time.

2011–12. At the end of the 2011 school year the JCPS superintendent's
contract was not renewed and a new superintendent was hired in the summer
of 2011. Seven new priority schools in JCPS were identified for the 2011–12
school year. Now there were thirteen. Ideally that would also mean an additional twenty-one education recovery staff. Problematically, the funds that
had paid for the first cohort of education recovery staff were school improvement funds from the Kentucky legislature. That line item had been zeroed out
and was no longer available.

The USDOE denied a request for the use of school SIG funds for the
memorandum of agreement arrangement that the state had for hiring ER staff
because it would be supplanting a process already in place. Dilemma. The
proposed solution was to hire a private educational staffing firm to contract
the ER staff still on an MOA but between the districts and the private group.

There were several reasons this did not play out in the state to be a
great idea, but in Jefferson the district indicated they wanted the ER staff
to be Jefferson employees rather than having an MOA. By the time that
arrangement was operationalized, it was almost time for school to begin
and the staffing could not be completed. In Kentucky, there is an informal
agreement that the state will not attempt to take teachers after the first month
of school from another district.

ERD Price took the staff that he had, assigning experienced ERLs to more
than one school and then spreading the remainder of ER staff (many of them
brand new to both education recovery and the district) among the schools
based on need. By year two, the ERLs had networked within the district to
know the people at the district level who could assist them in getting needed
data as well as meet other learning needs of students in the schools.

There were no formal trainings or meetings of all the ER staff in the district unique to them, but they attended turnaround trainings of the district and
ERLs attended the first portion of district principal meetings. Quality tools
other than the 30-60-90-day plans and quarterly reports were not a part of
requirements for use by ER staff in Jefferson, but the same networking that

was assisting ERLs with making connections in JCPS was also working with other ERs in other parts of the state. They began to share.

Mr. Price had begun conversations with the new superintendent regarding the barriers from protocols and procedures as well as the teacher contract for priority schools. Superintendent Dr. Donna Hargens was amenable to doing whatever it would take to make priority schools successful. At the end of year two ERD Price became superintendent in another district and Dr. Debbie Powers was hired in August 2012 to be the ERD in Jefferson.

2012–13. In Cohort 3 six new JCPS priority schools were identified. Now there were 19. This should mean that there were now 57 Education Recovery staff. Dr. Debbie Powers, who had been hired from the University of Louisville and had been working in JCPS schools for several years, was required to put her creative skills to work to serve the schools that had been in priority status for two years as well as the new ones. The 57 needed ER staff was closer to 30 at the beginning of school.

Very quickly ERD Powers and Superintendent Hargens began to meet regularly regarding the priority schools. Dr. Powers was included in cabinet-level meetings. Superintendent Hargens worked with the JCTA to remove barriers for teachers who were serving in priority schools. There was an obvious connection made among priority schools and the district. ER staff met together at least once every six weeks and the connections with U of L with graduate assistance and training were tightened.

The beginning of the JCPS collaboration with U of L, KDE and Jefferson with the National Institute for School Leadership occurred in this school year. Dr. Powers tightened up and clarified for all D180 the quarterly reporting format to make it ownable by schools.

2013–2017. No new priority schools were identified until 2014–15 when three elementary schools were added in JCPS. In 2016–17 an additional two schools were identified. Dr. Powers remained in the ERD role through May 2016 with focus on professional development and support for priority schools and collaboration at the district level. In addition, she was responsible for Trimble County High School, which would exit priority in three years.

Dr. Powers left the ERD role to work with the redesign of Stuart Middle School for Jefferson County schools. Superintendent Hargens resigned as superintendent in July 2017 after conducting a comprehensive planning process noted by the diagnostic review as a strength of the district. Many of the early barriers have been broken. It takes time. A director of priority schools has been added at the JCPS central office level to coordinate with the ERD the work to be done.

Conclusions: Progress and Struggles

Student assignment and restructuring of schools continue as issues. For example, one middle school has forty feeder elementary schools. Those forty feeder schools have multiple support systems they use with students. How can continuity occur? Some schools still have culture issues looming large. Until two years ago the high schools of origin were responsible for the accountability test scores of their students who were in alternative programs, thus making it almost impossible for school staff to see the impact of their own adjustments to curriculum, instruction, and support.

In 2015 at one of the priority high schools it was determined that of the graduating seniors only one-third of them had attended that high school all four years. With a focus on college and career readiness, some of the issues of mobility can be addressed, but it continues to be difficult to plan support for the students in the building when those students are very mobile.

In the work across the state, education recovery staff including JCPS ER staff receives training in the summer now including quality tools listed in this report as well as initiatives and strategies that are current best practice. The three region ERDs meet on a regular basis and there is growing alignment across the three regions regarding the model. In the summer of 2016 for the first time teachers from priority schools held workshops for teachers who are going to work in priority schools.

Tim Godbey who was a successful priority school principal was selected to be ERD for Jefferson in 2016. He has been able to begin a monthly walk-through process of priority schools with the school principal and district staff. This summary is an oversimplification of the struggle of D180 in serving priority schools in JCPS. Why would we share something that is so messy and with so much turnover among leadership? Why would we reflect on angst about how the model is supposed to work and did not sometimes? Angela Duckworth (University of Pennsylvania psychologist) might call it a lesson in grit.

Three schools in JCPS have exited priority status. Others have come close. In most priority schools progress is being made where goals are identified based on student data, strategies are in place, and teachers have the support to take risks and get better themselves. Continuous improvement is slow but becomes steady and sometimes leads to exponential growth when systems are built to withstand the turnover factors.

The systems are leadership, customer stakeholder focus, workforce focus, key core work processes, knowledge and information management, planning, and results. It is evident in some of the priority schools that they went to work on planning, customer stakeholder focus, and workforce focus systems first. It is evident in these schools that there is a plan for moving the school forward. So what happens when there is upheaval and turmoil? The system stays strong and adjusts if those in the system own it.

There is evidence all over the JCPS priority schools that these changes are occurring. Has it resulted in gap closure, math and literacy performance improvement, and college and career readiness? Yes, some, but not everywhere and not exponentially. There are still human issues.

Well, if D180 is such a great model, will it work in large urban districts? It can. If JCPS can be a lesson to be learned from, then implementing the model as designed with everyone who is to participate knowledgeable about it and then coached just in time when they need it would be the place to start before implementation.

If an urban district were to

- have a clear vision for its students/schools based on who they are and where they want to be/go/do,
- underpin the vision with an actionable strategic plan,
- align with school improvement plans to get the work done,
- build with interventions for the students assigned to that school

and if

- every person in the district is knowledgeable on an operational level of how his or her work aligns to meet the goals for the intended results,
- every person has just in time support available for his or her own professional capacity building,
- every level is encouraged to build leaders to assist in closest to the student decision making,
- interested vendors and funders are required to show how what they must offer will assist in accomplishing the items before funding applications were written, and
- once resources are made available based on need, plans aligned, and monitored, then models such as D180 should and can work.

KEY IDEAS

- Nothing is linear. There is not a prescribed solution to each set of circumstances.
- Not all tools work in every situation, every time—flexibility and agility are necessary.
- Be certain the people sent to help have the capacity to do so.
- Never give up.

Chapter 9

Lessons Learned and Continued Challenges

Based on Kentucky work specifically and continuous improvement work generally, the following lessons can be easily identified and learned.

If schools and districts could solve the problems on their own, they already would have.

Just as in all schools, in low-performing schools people work long hours and have tough days just getting through to students. Professionals have a heart for students and the work. Coming from different experiences and backgrounds, hired at different times and with various funds, individuals are hired to work with students to do a specific job.

Often in low-performing schools educators and the community are overwhelmed by the external factors, the conflicting local policies and politics, and the differences in their own training. Often there has been little effort to create coordinating teams simply because the daily fires to be put out are great, emotional, and hot.

As the current national trend for educational thinking now is, allowing the problems to be solved locally should not be a debate. Who knows the students better than the people teaching them? Who knows better how to work with local parents and stakeholders than local people? Problematically, those same people may not have the common training necessary or the common planning for strategies and best practices that could result in improved student achievement for the students they need to serve. Even if they have the training, implementation tends to be random.

Once systems theory and continuous process improvement is embraced, the common language can pull the individuals into a powerful force for their own professional improvement and ultimately improvement of student performance. If priority work has taught us lessons, one of the greatest is that common language, common processes, problem solving, and empowerment through relationship building make the difference. Can schools do that without state help? Certainly they can, and yet many have not. Quality, trained, visionary, collaborative leadership with targeted goals is crucial.

No matter what the political climate, uniqueness is evidenced at the school and classroom level.

The dynamics and requirements may change. Laws may change. A well-designed and implemented system can adjust. All systems have a governance structure. All systems have customer and stakeholder requirements. All systems require strategies for improvement. All systems have common key core work processes in curriculum and instruction. All components require coaching. All systems have professional learning and support to be successful and all systems will have results. In addition, all systems must determine how to use the knowledge and information within the system.

Look to what is in existence to see which components need to be improved on and are not getting the intended results. For example, as the agency began to look at closing the achievement gaps in Kentucky, it was clear that many legislators believed there needed to be new laws to approach the gap. A research of existing law showed that there were over forty laws that addressed achievement gaps. It was not a new law that was needed but an understanding of where the current laws were not being enforced or whether the current laws were addressing the gap. That had to be the starting place.

In any given school when starting to look at any given issue, once the issue is identified, what are the current processes and plans in place and what about them is not working? By always looking to the process, redundancy can be eliminated. There often are multiple laws or plans in place already. Where do they fit in the system and what about them is not working? There is seldom a need to start over. Give people credit for the work they have already done and build from there.

At a recent Kentucky Board of Education (August 2017) meeting, a familiar mantra was repeated: "Surely people throughout the country have decided what best practice is and are doing it. We need to see what they are doing. We can't expect to get different results from the same processes." Absolutely true and yet many other areas are looking to Kentucky about turnaround. What works for students in a school depends on all the work processes mentioned. It really is not something from outside until organizations diagnose their own systems for these work processes. Two-way partnerships can assist with the outside stories in best practice too.

Once effective systems are built for the key core work processes, the systems learn to respond to the political climate or environment of the day and not come completely undone even if names, people, and statutes change.

With the 2015 election in Kentucky, the governorship changed from a Democratic to a Republican leader. In the Kentucky legislature the membership moved from a majority Democratic house and Republican senate to both chambers being majority Republican. There was a new commissioner of education, Dr. Stephen Pruitt, hired in the fall of 2015. Ideologies regarding charter schools and involvement of the Department of Education in support for interventions in schools and districts changed.

The key core work processes are still the same. Yet there has not needed to be a wholesale removal of all state education employees because the operational system components are the same. As laws change and regulations are promulgated they can still be administered through continuous improvement structures. It is not the people alone but the people working in well-defined system categories that make the difference.

From 1990 to 2009 to 2017, major legislation has called for various iterations of the laws, but the core processes continue to hold structures. This does not imply that there can be no change, but there can be an approach to address the change in the system for continuous improvement.

At the same August Kentucky board meeting referenced earlier a board member asked how KDE knows that the proficiency that we are shooting for with all students is employability. Good question. By having a fluid stakeholder input process on major issues and decisions, the stakeholders/shareholders and organizations supporting education should be able to predict how a change will impact the overall system and potentially the cost. How novel!

It is the responsibility of educational leaders to work with political leaders and stakeholders/shareholders for clarity and understanding of what the data and information are telling us and then guide them from abstract ideologies to actions that can create the intended outcomes for the systems.

Political leaders arrive at their conclusions from varied inputs. Sometimes it is a political party platform that is adhered to faithfully with no question. Sometimes it is a constituency priority that the politician has been elected to address. Sometimes the politician is married to an educator or he or she is/was an educator. Sometimes the politician just has a great idea about how schools should be. All those ideologies meld together to create law. One of the things that Commissioner Holliday did that assisted District 180 was to work from the very beginning of his time as commissioner with politicians to understand what District 180 needed to be and that it was the practical application of SB1 (2009).

When pushback occurred from those who were representing the districts where schools had been identified for participation, there was not a lack of clarity of how the practical application had come about. The common goal was to get all Kentucky students to college and career readiness, and this is what it would take for priority (District 180) schools.

Kentucky education is fortunate to have many stakeholder groups to support schools. They each have a purpose for being an organization ensuring that an aspect of the organization is always considered. The message that the commissioner cultivated with the K groups as they are known was college and career readiness for all of Kentucky's children. The easy system question is: How does what you are doing/asking help us help students become college and career ready? Very focused.

Key K groups are: Kentucky Association of School Superintendents (KASS), Kentucky School Boards Association (KSBA), Kentucky Association of School Administrators (KASA), Kentucky Association of School Councils (KASC), Kentucky Education Association (KEA), Kentucky Association for Gifted Education (KAGE), Kentucky Center for School Safety (KCSS), and Kentucky High School Athletic Association (KHSAA).

Not a K group but equally important is the Prichard Committee for Academic Excellence. Started in the 1980s as a government group providing recommendations for improvement, the Prichard members reconstituted themselves as a private nonprofit pushing for excellence in all areas and in all levels of public education. They have been and are a force and rational voice in public education in Kentucky.

Leadership at every level of each system must have just in time training and be empowered to make decisions closest to their level of work.

Each leader and worker must understand clearly why things are happening based on what information and data are available to build relationships for common goals. Leaders must model what they want to see using tools to design and deploy systems aligning resources as they go. There must be no fear of retribution for taking risks. There must be support and training just in time when leaders themselves are struggling.

For example, in the priority schools, the D180 model gave a day in and day out coach for the principal and for literacy and math teachers. Ideally those people were the best people available to provide just in time, nonthreatening, problem-solving support to improve the systems of leadership (governance) and instruction (teaching). An education recovery director was put in place to provide just in time, nonthreatening, problem-solving support to improve the education recovery system for ER school staff supporting the schools.

An associate commissioner was assigned among other duties to provide just in time, nonthreatening, problem-solving support to improve the overall system of D180 through education recovery director support. The belief was that the model would build relationships that would influence teacher/student relationships that were just in time, nonthreatening, and problem-solving support. Once teachers are empowered and empower students, as a grandmother would say, "Katy, bar the door!"

Reality is that funding was always an issue from the beginning to provide adequate staffing for D180. In the three-year growth of adding thirty-one more schools to the original ten, ER staff should have grown to 123 and reduced as schools came out of priority status. At its height, the most ever employed in any given year was seventy. In year two, as the issue of supplanting was being a barrier with the USDOE, all staff had to be reinterviewed through a district by district policy. Jefferson County hired its own education recovery staff. Under union contract conditions, a new level of collaboration had to occur with the Department of Education to allow for specific priority training.

The uncertainty brought turnover. Turnover in the ER staff and keeping them trained is an issue. Even so, many of the education recovery alums are now superintendents, principals, amazing classroom teachers, and district office leaders in multiple districts in Kentucky applying continuous improvement strategies and tools. The people who come on board annually to ER find a supportive environment in other ERs or they do not stay. Training and coaching never stop. Leaders at all levels must be able to create the systems that can work.

Key leaders must believe that dramatic, sustainable, continuous improvement can be done.

Communication and the message must be transparent and support steadily given. Leaders must be willing to give up position, self, power, and the role of manager and decision maker to empower people to build aligned systems. The "yeah, but" mentality must be gone. "We believe that all students should be college and career ready." "Yeah, but our kids are poor." "The teachers are not trained well enough. Parents do not care." Etc.

Instead the conversation must be that "we believe and our actions show that all students will be college and career ready." With the new accountability system in Kentucky the term may be transition ready. Terms do not matter as much as clarity of purpose. After purpose is clarified take the laws, regulations, and best practices and work with the people available to create the highest performing systems educators can with the resources they have.

It is far easier to get outside assistance when the system is so clearly defined that the funding source understands how their monies will be used and how they will help meet the goal. It creates more collaborative communities too.

For example, in one of the Eastern Kentucky schools, the attendance rate was about 85 percent. The ERD asked them what they did about attendance. They told her that letters went home at certain intervals and students could be referred to the court system. She asked how the court system handled it. They told her that they seldom got much help from the courts. Then she asked them how they prepared to go to court. With a quizzical look they asked her what she meant. She said, "When you take a student/parents to court for attendance what do you take with you?"

They indicated they took a printout of the attendance. She asked if they had evidence of what they had done to intervene with the parents. They stared at her and said that it was not required. She then said, "I bet that if you have a detailed process for attendance in the school to include who called when, what conversations were had, and what has occurred and take it to the judge consistently every time, you will get a different reaction."

When schools and districts clean up everything about a system within their control, others recognize that work. The ERD suggested they give a judge a call and ask him or her what it would take to have better outcomes. Because the local judge graduated from the high school, he was very willing to have the conversation. This "yeah, but" about the court system changed simply by looking at a system in the building.

Training and solutions must come just in time. Nothing really matters until it matters. Training in August that is not directly related to something an educator does or maybe will not do until December will not have the same degree of engagement as just in time support does.

The concept of the hub schools that has been developed since 2013 is to have schools that have been through continuous improvement just in time training and have improved systems to be able to share with other schools in the state on a just in time basis. Normally educators do that through presentations at a conference or early release days. The hub is a school operating all the time. Other schools are encouraged to visit the school in action.

Hub work is very focused on the needs of the people visiting. Primarily the sharing is built around the tools found in part III of this book. Since 2013, 3,100 educators have visited the hub schools (appendix F).

Sustainability in leadership must be planned and coached.

State leadership must also be coached. Fortunately, the commissioner employing the Eastern Kentucky ERD turned interim associate commissioner could encourage her to stay around to be coach for the new associate commissioner. Sustainability requires that the person who comes next understands the processes that are negotiable and the ones that are essential to continuous improvement in that office and in the work.

D180 was in an office with Title I, alternative education, instructional technology, community relations, school improvement planning, and implementation of approximately sixty state laws. Then there was how the bureaucracy worked and the realization that there were six other offices at KDE. The new associate was scheduled time to discuss the work with those other associates. Kevin Brown, Hiren Desai, David Couch, Felicia Smith, Ken Draut, and Dale Winkler were crucial relationships to be built very quickly because priority work was not the only work of the agency.

State departments of education must take the lead in moving from compliance to effectiveness through modeling efficient systems. Aligned communication is critical. Singular messaging with one voice about priority work had to happen. As Mr. Fred Rogers would say, "Look for the helpers." Other associates were key as well as relationships with Mary Ann Miller (the commissioner's administrator), Lisa Gross, and Rebecca Blessing (communications).

As the new associate began to work, the just in time coach supported her activities with daily reviews of processes, ongoing PDSAs, planning of things already being developed like the collaboration with AdvancED for the first continuous improvement summit or implementation of hub schools, or how to handle the calls with USDOE on principle 2 of the waiver of NCLB.

About six months after the ERD turned associate turned coach left Kentucky, she was asked to return to fill an interim position in another office. This was an opportunity to use the same quality tools discussed in part III in that office to address issues and hire the new associate.

The hiring process for the associate commissioner for the Office of Next Generation Professionals enabled a collaboration to begin between the D180 associate and the successful candidate, Dr. Amanda Ellis, which continues to this day. All these opportunities enabled a mentor/coaching relationship primarily behind D180 and continuous improvement to occur for almost four more years.

Could those associate commissioners have made the transition to their roles without coaching? Surely. It happens all the time. What is more important is that they did not have to build new processes but instead improve using tools that were beginning to be understood in the agency as well as in the field. PDSA is now a continuous improvement term common among agency conversations.

KEY IDEAS

- Building sustainable systems for continuous improvement yielding amazing student and educator experiences in the Commonwealth and anywhere else learning takes place is dynamic, not static, and completely challenging.
- Improvement can be and is being done.
- There must be a sense of urgency behind systems management theory in education for continuous improvement if American education is to meet the challenges for all its children.
- The blame game and "I have to be right" environment in educational conversation is over.
- Encouraging things are happening right now, without trumpets.

Appendix A

LCHS Sustainability Plan

(When a school exits priority status, the sustainability plan is monitored by ERD for one year.)

Roles	*Current Personnel*
Principal	Fill in names
Assistant Principals	Fill in names
Counselors	Fill in names
Academic Performance Consultant (APC)	Fill in names
Administrative Team	Fill in names
School Media Specialist	Fill in names
Athletic Director	Fill in names
Administrative Secretary	Fill in names
Twenty-First Century Director	Fill in names
School Technology Coordinator	Fill in names
Central Office (CO) Staff	Fill in names
Communication to responsible parties: All parties mentioned in this document collaborated to create it and are aware of their roles in the sustainability plan.	

Sustainable Areas	Person Responsible	Beginning Date	Status Check	Time Frames
Academic and Instruction Administrative Team				
Assessment Calendar	Fill in names	Current responsibility	When was the assessment calendar last updated? How often do teachers receive IC updates?	September: assessment calendar finalized and communicated to all staff.
IC				
Failure Rates	Fill in names	Current responsibility	How often are the data reviewed currently?	Analyzed monthly; reported monthly to administrative team.
Dropout Rates	Fill in names	Current responsibility	How often are the data reviewed currently?	Analyzed monthly; reported monthly to administrative team.

Sustainable Areas	Person Responsible	Beginning Date	Status Check	Time Frames
Parent Involvement (Title I)	Fill in names	Current responsibility	How will LCHS communicate with families? How will two-way communication be implemented and utilized?	When new initiatives are introduced, a parent academy will be organized and scheduled to inform families. Representatives from the administrative team will present new initiatives to the school board during working sessions to inform leadership stakeholders. School Messenger, Facebook, Instagram, and the school webpage will be utilized to share information with parents. Surveys, open house events, and school email will be utilized to provide families an opportunity to provide feedback to the school. Title I: each school to annually review (and revise if needed) the parent involvement policy and parent-student-teacher compacts.
Novice Reduction	Fill in names	Beginning October 2015, full rollout January 2016	How will this be introduced to staff? Will there be training involved?	Soft rollout scheduled for October 2015. Novice reduction targets received in November 2015. Statewide rollout January 2016.

Sustainable Areas	Person Responsible	Beginning Date	Status Check	Time Frames
Persistence to Graduation/ Removing Barriers to Education	Fill in names	Current responsibility	How often are the data reviewed currently? What is being done to address poor attendance of students?	Data is analyzed weekly during Monday meetings, home visits are scheduled, weekly updates from the team. Persistence to graduation tools are utilized to remove barriers to education. FRYSC services and local assistance services are provided to students.
Graduation Rate	Fill in names	Current responsibility	How often are the data reviewed currently?	Analyzed monthly; reported monthly to administrative team.
Program Reviews	Fill in names	Monthly, during Wednesday PLC meetings. Full review and feedback by administrative team bimonthly.	Stacy will organize and work with team leads to complete tasks. The administrative team will review and give feedback.	Monthly review and status check all.
Study Island (Instructional Use)	Fill in names	Current responsibility	Currently SI is being paid for out of SIG funds, but local and federal monies will be used for purchase when the current agreement expires in 2017. LCHS receives approximately $23,000 in Title I funds each year.	Study Island has been purchased by Edmentum and we have a multiyear contract with that company paid through the SIG grant.

Sustainable Areas	Person Responsible	Beginning Date	Status Check	Time Frames
Gifted	Fill in names	How is this monitored to ensure individual plans are met? What are the reporting requirements (monthly, annually, other)?		Ensure a clear plan for meeting and monitoring that identified student needs are met.
Weekly Tutoring through Twenty-First Century	Fill in names	Will the current process continue (that is, change in number of days available each week)?		Need to improve how assignments and feedback are returned to teachers.
ASSIST	Fill in names	Uploaded 30-60-90 notes, progress notes, CSIP, DR requirements, and gap report.		Training needed as both are new to LCHS. DR self-assessment due September 2015. CSIP due January 2016.
CERT	Fill in names	Monitor for implementation and gain feedback from teachers.		Ninth and tenth grade will test two times, eleventh grade will test three times.
Plan Book	Fill in names	Teachers voted to utilize the plan book program for this year.		Garner feedback from staff at the end of the year (May 2016) to determine if plan book should be utilized next year.

Sustainable Areas	Person Responsible	Beginning Date	Status Check	Time Frames
Student Mentoring (Link Crew)	Fill in names	New program this year. How are students with mentoring needs identified? How is this being monitored? How often? What are the reporting requirements to measure success?		Need system in place to ensure mentoring is efficient, effective, and implemented.
ARC Chairperson	Fill in names	What are time demands? What are time requirements for the Special Education Department chair? What PD is needed to support the regular/special education co-teaching model?		Ensure high expectations for all students and that all students have equal opportunities to curriculum.

Sustainable Areas	Person Responsible	Beginning Date	Status Check	Time Frames
Data Analysis Data Collection	Fill in names	January 2016	How are longitudinal student data being collected and analyzed? When is the district quarterly report due date/format (new after exiting priority)? Monitor data analysis forms in all PLC groups and follow up implementation for RTI. Identify intervention groups.	Quarterly report aligned with district time frame/format. Quarterly reports are due October 9, 2015, December 1, 2015, March 1, 2016, and June 1, 2016. PLC meetings during data analysis.
ESS/Intervention Tab Reporting	Fill in names	Current responsibility	Who will identify students for math and reading intervention by ESS teachers?	As required: Initial identification of targeted students; review in January of students that need to be pulled from elective classes; entering students; monitoring of ALEKS and reading plus students.
Summer School ~Designing ~Reporting ~Budget			Who will be the *one* person to oversee summer school and ensure it is implemented. Who reports to KDE?	Implementation and consistent reporting to KDE.
Grades ~ Standards-Based Grading Implementation ~Posting to IC ~Monitoring Student	Fill in names	Current responsibility (with support from counselors)	How are we addressing this improvement? Priority as identified in the March 2014 Diagnostic Review Report? SBG. Is standards-based grading being implemented with fidelity?	Need process for monitoring implementation of standards-based grading, monitoring of grades, follow up with teachers not following protocol.

Advance KY ~Reimbursements ~Courses	Fill in names	Current responsibility	Follow Advance KY guidelines.	Follow Advance KY guidelines. *Be sure to request all reimbursements by November 1.
Student Data Notebooks	Fill in names	Current responsibility	Who is creating and copying pages for data notebooks? How are data notebooks monitored?	Purchase any needed supplies; prepare materials prior to beginning of school; review data notebooks protocol and make needed changes; monitor data notebooks and provide feedback.
Writing ~Implement Writing Plan	Fill in names	Current responsibility (this is a new position and continues to be developed around student/ staff need)	Is the district writing plan being visited on a regular basis with staff? Is there a policy or procedure in place that supports the writing plan and outlines the school protocol? Do teachers understand their roles in implementing the writing plan?	The writing plan is revisited bimonthly in Wednesday PLC meetings. Each department is required to develop a plan for implementation of the district writing plan. During January 2016 "data day" with staff, writing coach will review OD scores and ensure communication of writing plan. Maintain the timeline for meeting deadlines.
LEAD Report	Fill in names	Current responsibility	What needs to be confirmed to complete the LEAD report?	
School Safety				

Area		Current responsibility	Questions	System/Notes
Discipline Referrals / School Behavior	Fill in names	Current responsibility	How are we recognizing positive behavior? Are all staff aware of the PBIS plan and expectations, roles, and responsibilities?	PBIS committee has been established and meets regularly to review data and target students for behavioral intervention. Student handbook clearly outlines student code of conduct.
Safety Drills and Reporting	Fill in names	Current responsibility	How are required monthly drills being scheduled? Are reporting dates being met?	
Building Cleanliness/ Custodians	Fill in names	Current responsibility	What system is in place to monitor and check daily building cleanliness? Do custodians know their roles/responsibilities and what monitoring is in place?	Regular and consistent monitoring and upkeep.
Maintenance Requests	Fill in names	Current responsibility	Is there a system in place? Do all staff know what that system is? What action needs to be taken to ensure that staff members are following protocols?	Develop/use requisition form or reporting system for timely submission/action.
Field Trips/Bus Requests	Fill in names	Current responsibility	Is funding in place?	Approval system in place to quality control academic need.
Extra Duty Rosters/ Assignments	Fill in names	Current responsibility	Is there a system for monitoring? How are those not reporting for duty being addressed?	System for monitoring staff on duty or have a replacement in critical areas.

Emergency Procedures: • Medical Conditions • Collecting Emergency • Student/Staff Data • Entry into IC Technology	Fill in names	Current responsibility	Who is sending home emergency forms at the beginning of the year? Who is monitoring the process for new/transfer students?	Is there a more efficient way of collecting this information than the current system? Explore for 2016–17.
School Plan and Needs Assessment	Fill in names	Current responsibility	Has a school technology plan been developed and communicated with all staff members?	Ensure all technology is monitored, maintained, and utilized appropriately.
Training and Maintenance	Fill in names	Current responsibility	How are staff members being trained to utilize available technology with students? Is student use being monitored?	This position will be contingent on technology availability following reconstruction after the fire. Ensure teachers allow students access.
School Culture Administrative and Turnaround Teams				
Celebrating Successes (Student, Staff, Community)	Fill in names	Current responsibility (needs consistency, particularly attendance rewards)	What action needs to be taken to ensure that dates/celebrations are established?	System for ensuring celebrations are planned for students for attendance, behavior, CCR, assessments, etc.
Parent Involvement and Parent/Student Support Title I	Fill in names	Current responsibility	What survey or plan is there to see how parents want to be involved? How will involvement be addressed next year?	When new initiatives are introduced, a parent academy will be organized and scheduled to inform.

			Assessments? Who will analyze results and ensure implementation?	Will present new initiatives to the school board during working sessions to inform leadership stakeholders. School Messenger, Facebook, Instagram, and the school webpage will be utilized to share information with parents. Surveys, open house events, and school email will be utilized to provide families an opportunity to provide feedback to the school. Title I requires each school to annually review (and revise if needed) the parent involvement policy and parent-student-teacher compacts.
Communication ~Newsletter ~Website ~Parent Group ~Alert System ~School Sign	Fill in names	Current responsibility	What opportunities are available for two-way communication between school and stakeholder groups?	Delegate responsibilities as needed (that is, club sponsors, patriot coaches, athletic coaches, etc.).
Student Handbook	Fill in names	Current responsibility	What changes need to be made to the handbook?	Ensure all changes are included, particularly standards-based grading as well as any policy changes.

Patriot Time/Clubs	Fill in names	Current responsibility	What changes need to be made to reduce loss of instructional time and still allow students this time?	Ensure planning is taking place to maximize the time allocated.
Hospitality	Fill in names	Beginning in Fall 2015.	Who will be attending? How many will be attending? Who is sending the invitation? What is needed? What is the time frame?	Hospitality is important to ensure stakeholders feel welcome in our building and an important part of our school community.
Athletics	Fill in names	Current responsibility	How does the athletic program support the academic program?	
School Council Budget Plan and Monitoring (Local and Federal)	Fill in names	Current responsibility	Prioritize school improvement needs utilizing 30-60-90-day plans, needs assessments, and academic data.	The school's right to establish a council or the school's right for the council to assume the full authority granted under KRS 160.345 shall be restored if the school is not classified as persistently low achieving for two (2) consecutive years.
School Council/ Council Policies	Fill in names	Current responsibility (shift from advisory to council)	What policies need to be developed/revised/reviewed? Program review? Writing policy?	Ensure all policies are in place. Policies are reviewed yearly (during the summer months) to ensure compliance and effective support of school instructional program.
Council Committee Assignments	Fill in names	Current responsibility	What are the roles/ responsibilities of committees in addition to program reviews?	Develop monthly agenda for each committee meeting to follow to ensure committees are functioning properly and efficiently.

Instructional Leadership				
Day-to-Day Operations	Fill in names	Current responsibility	What roles will change due to decreased staffing (SAM, etc.)?	Identify roles/responsibilities that will need to be assigned with loss of staff.
PLC Meetings ~ELA ~Math ~Science ~Social Studies ~A&H ~PLCS	Fill in names	Current responsibility	Which administrator is assigned to each department? Is the assigned administrator attending PLC meetings including after school? Are minutes and agendas turned in monthly to a designated person?	Need a process for school leadership to monitor PLC meetings regularly to ensure that data notebooks are maintained, data are analyzed, analysis is used to address student learning, program review requirements are addressed consistently and ongoing, and the writing plan is being followed.
Reports (30, 60, 90; Quarterly Report, School Report Card)	Fill in names	Current responsibility	What system is in place to ensure all staff report in a timely manner and follow up for implementation? Should these dates be included on shared school calendar?	Begin completing the district quarterly report in conjunction with KDE quarterly reporting requirements. Current due dates are October 9, December 1, March 1, and June 1.

Walkthrough Schedule, Documentation, Follow Up	Fill in names	Current responsibility	Is there a schedule for walkthrough collection? Is there a process to identify and correct walkthrough deficiencies with staff? Do the assigned walkthroughs correlate to lesson plan checks or is there another process? How do we calibrate "rigorous" instruction? Is rigor defined and understood by all staff?	At LCHS, administrators and APCs will complete five walkthroughs weekly and discuss findings during weekly administrative meetings. All walkthrough data should be followed with feedback within the walkthrough document (ELEOT) and, whenever necessary, face-to-face conversation (walkthrough without documented feedback/follow up will not produce change). District team currently has three walkthrough cycles each year with a debriefing meeting and feedback report for each cycle for each school.
School Improvement Plan	Fill in names	Current responsibility	Do staff members understand the connection between thirty-day reports and CSIP?	Continue to help staff see the connection between the CSIP and the thirty-day plans. New CSIP is due in ASSIST January 1. Continue to help department drill down to areas that need improvement by providing models, examples, and other tools to guide the development of CSIP/thirty-day plans.

Category				
Content Curriculum	Fill in names	Current responsibility	When will curriculum be reviewed for changes? What assistance do they need? Is the curriculum offered for all students challenging and equitable?	Ensure all content curriculum documents are reviewed annually.
Mission/Vision/ Belief Statements	Fill in names	Current responsibility	Are mission/vision/belief statements revisited annually with stakeholders? Are they communicated regularly and consistently?	Ensure mission/vision/belief statements processes are formalized in policy/ practice involving stakeholders.
Systems Approach	Fill in names	Current responsibility	Are plus/deltas being used effectively? Are deltas addressed promptly? Are all content areas using systems in their PLC meetings?	Ensure systems are implemented, monitored, and follow-up action is taken consistently and regularly.
Assessment and Data Building Assessment Coordinator (BAC)	Fill in names	Current responsibility	What assistance is needed by BAC? Who responds to needs?	Ensure school leadership assists BAC with classroom walkthrough; scheduling for both testing and nontesting groups; other needs as BAC requests.
Testing Accommodation	Fill in names	Current responsibility	How many students need accommodations? How many staff members will be needed to provide accommodations?	Ensure accommodation code training has been completed. Ensure all teachers are aware of accommodated testing schedule.

End of Course (EOC)	Fill in names	Current responsibility	Who is monitoring benchmark data on common assessments at the school level? In sub-PLCs? In department meetings?	Ensure applicable departments develop common assessment schedule for interims. End of course data is monitored after each common assessment, each interim assessment, and following each grade report. Students who are struggling may be placed in a strategies class, red zone intervention, or ESS tutoring. Also, due to our standards-based grading policy, students are provided multiple opportunities to demonstrate learning. We have several safety nets in place to ensure students success. Determination for the EOC assessment is made on a student by student basis.

Intervention Classes (Strategies Classes)	Fill in names	Current responsibility	Once counselors identify students who need interventions, who will facilitate focusing on individual skills? Monitor implementation of interventions? Can ESS teachers assist to facilitate interventions? Who can take over responsibility of creating rosters in reading plus and ALEKS?	Ensure a proactive plan is in place by teachers for students needing interventions (assigning to classes is just the beginning).
Career Readiness	Fill in names	Current responsibility	Are new factors being identified to identify students at career reading (that is, replacement of COMPASS test)?	Ensure pathways are identified and entered correctly into TEDS.
KOSSA	Fill in names	Current responsibility	Are individual skill sets developed to meet KOSSA requirements?	Ensure pathways are identified and entered correctly into TEDS.
Work Keys	Fill in names	Current responsibility	Who is identifying students who need to take work keys?	Ensure interventions are being provided for students to be better prepared and familiar with testing format.
ASVAB	Fill in names	Current responsibility	Are there skills that need to be addressed to facilitate student success on ASVAB? Who has this responsibility?	Ensure interventions are being provided for students to be better prepared and familiar with testing format.

College Readiness	Fill in names	Current responsibility	How can twelfth-grade teachers assist in facilitating college readiness?	Monitor effectiveness of college readiness courses to ensure they are meeting the needs of students.
Individual Learning Plans (ILPs)	Fill in names	Current responsibility	ILP responsibilities are shared with identified content teachers by grade level.	Monitoring of deadlines to ensure ILPs are completed in a timely manner. The ILP career planner is a required component for all CTE classes. CTE teachers are required to utilize the ILP resources monthly. Usage is tracked through student completion rates.
Additional Assessments ~Grade ~AP Exams ~Interims	Fill in names	Current responsibility	Which assessments are mandatory? Which assessments are requested by teachers? What is the testing window? How many times will these assessments be administered?	Monitor how data are used to make instructional decisions based on PLC data analysis protocols.
Graduation	Fill in names	Current responsibility	How will responsibility for task completion be disseminated among senior patriot coaches? Is there a written protocol for graduation?	Monitor to ensure all required graduation tasks are completed in a timely manner (that is, cap and gown orders, senior trip guidelines, monitor senior grades, finalize graduating senior list).

Professional Development

Item	Names	Responsibility	Questions	Notes
Needs Assessments	Fill in names	Current responsibility	Does staff understand how to complete a survey utilizing Survey Monkey? Is there a survey available that we currently use to determine PD needs?	Use Survey Monkey to gather needs assessment periodically throughout the year, with a final survey at the end of the year to determine needs for following school year.
PD Plan		Current responsibility	What PD is needed to support initiatives? Improvement goals in CSIP and thirty-day plans?	Identify PD needs annually, but also quarterly as new initiatives begin.
Staff PD	Fill in names	Current responsibility	What needs have been identified based on the needs assessment? Is there anyone "in house" who can provide training and support?	PD needs assessment is administered near the end of each school year. Analyze needs assessment to determine overall staff needs and develop schoolwide PD plan from this assessment. Utilize individual professional growth plans to determine professional development needs of individual teachers. Also review walkthrough data to determine trend needs (management, technology, etc.).
PD Log	Fill in names	Current responsibility	Will CIITS continue to be utilized to track and record PD or will a new system be developed?	Currently Mr. Ward enters PD into CIITS, but consider training the school receptionist to complete this task.
PGES				

Category				
Self-Reflections, Professional Growth Plans, and Student Growth Goals	Fill in names	Current responsibility	Planning templates have been created to assist teachers in completing self-reflections and PGPs.	Meet district timelines; all components due in CIITS by October 1.
Implementation and Training	Fill in names	Current responsibility	Training materials are available for updates and new staff training.	Provide "workshops" for veteran teachers. Monitor to ensure timelines are being met.
Accuracy and Calibration of Data	Fill in names	Current responsibility	Calibration training required.	Evaluating administrators will attend CEP update training and complete TeachScape calibration training as required.
New Teachers ~Orientation ~Mentoring (New Teachers and Those Needing Assistance)	Fill in names	Current responsibility	Are new teachers receiving support other than KTIP? Are mentors assigned within the building?	Recommend new teachers to receive initial orientation at the school level and regular guidance regarding standards-based grading, program reviews, programs related to content, CIITS, etc. The district provides new teacher orientation that includes a full day in the summer and four, two-hour sessions during the school year.

Appendix B

30-60-90-Day Plan

Leslie County High School: Each school chose three main ideas (big rocks) around which to build the plans. The following example is a year plan for only one rock, that of school culture. Academic performance and data-based decision making were the other two topics (rocks) selected and plans will be made available through the authors. This was Leslie's first plan during her first year, about ninety days in. Each thirty-day plan was reviewed and turned to green type if on track, yellow if moving forward but not where it needs to be, and red if it needed to be reworked. All 150 days were in a general outline working back from the goal for the rock. Details for the next thirty days were filled in each thirty days when the plan was reviewed.

Big Rock A: School Culture—Vision

In the first thirty days, we will know we are successful when:

The school has created clearly defined mission and vision statements, utilizing a collaborative approach involving wide stakeholder representation. (Was completed by the thirty-day review [green].)

The measures/evidences we will use are: minutes and agenda of faculty meeting where school staff input regarding mission and vision is sought (green); minutes and agenda of stakeholder meeting (parents, students, area stakeholders) with the same purpose of above faculty meeting (green); and the existence of clearly defined mission and vision statements (green).

First Thirty Days Action Strategies	Who is on point?	How will we communicate it?
A1. The school will reconvene the transformation team to develop and define the vision statement as well as revisit the mission statement. This is designed to take advantage of the infrastructure previously established during the creation of the SIG to seek stakeholder input. Held August 12 (green).	Team names here	The local newspaper will be invited to the visioning meeting to be able to publicize the school's process of updating the mission and vision (specific person name to arrange all for August 12 meeting) (green).
A2. The school will meet with the faculty on the opening day of school to seek input from them as to mission and vision. This information will be considered as well as student input when the final statements are developed. Statements posted (green).	PLC chairs, principal, ERD	The school's mission and vision will be posted in all classrooms as well as commons areas to benefit staff, students, and visitors.
A3. The school will provide opportunities for teachers in PLCs to provide additional input on mission and vision (was done in small groups) (green).	PLC chairs, principal, ERD	The principal will train PLC facilitators on the process of leading the members of their PLC to brainstorm ideas to possibly include in the mission and vision (green).

Sixty Days Action Strategies (Color notation indicates sixty-day review)	Who is on point?	How will we communicate it?
A4. The school will seek input from students during RTI/enrichment block regarding mission and vision. In addition to being able to seek input from students, this will also provide a deliberate opportunity to begin the marketing campaign with students to embed value of mission and vision and their role in making the mission and vision a reality (green). If we are not successful, we will: Restructure the process after determining the barriers to successful development of mission and vision. In sixty days, we will know we are successful when: Eighty percent of stakeholders can clearly articulate the mission and vision of the school. The measures/evidences we will use are: A stakeholder survey assessing their ability to articulate the mission and vision of the school. An intentional effort will be made to create surveys that are uniquely able to solicit quality input from each stakeholder group. Aggregate data from the above survey.	Principal, assistant principal, counselors, block teachers	The principal with support of the ERL will train the faculty on the process with which to gain input from the student body and meetings will be conducted (green).
A5. The school will develop and distribute a school mission/vision survey (green).	ER team	The survey will be distributed to faculty (green) and students via SharePoint. Parent input on the survey will come through a hard copy of the survey being sent home to every student. The survey will also be published in the local newspaper (yellow).

A6. The school will host a culture audit facilitated by the staff of Kentucky Valley Educational Cooperative (KVEC). Results will give the school additional corroborating evidence of school stakeholders' ability to clearly articulate and internalize the school's mission and vision (completed by October) (green).

If we are not successful, we will:

Examine the mission and vision survey results to ascertain specifically which stakeholder group(s) are the least able to clearly articulate the school's mission and vision and then restructure our media campaign approach to target selected stakeholder groups.

In ninety days, we will know we are successful when:

Ninety-five percent of stakeholders can clearly articulate the mission and vision of the school.

School staff are internalizing the school's mission and vision and are implementing elements of the school's mission and vision statements into their daily activities.

The measures/evidence we will use are:

Redistributed school mission and vision survey

School walkthrough data

Anecdotal data provided through interviews

Ninety Days Action Strategies

A8. Redistribute the school's mission and vision survey. Faculty will meet to analyze the student survey and create a plan for the next steps to ensure student understanding (students given survey in October, results not yet distributed) (yellow).

Specific names included district-level contact, KVEC

The school's goal is for all stakeholders to be able to clearly articulate the school's mission and vision (mixed green and yellow).

Who is on point?
Specific names here

How will we communicate it?
Based on the data gathered from the initial survey, the leadership team will disaggregate the data and redistribute the survey to those target groups whose ability to articulate is not clear (yellow).

120 Days Action Strategies	Who is on point?	How will we communicate it?
A9. The school will provide feedback to teachers in PLCs as to the results of the KVEC culture audit. The purpose is to continue to empower teachers with the information they need to internalize the key components of the school's mission and vision (green).	ER/principal	The school principal with support of the ERL will provide the culture audit results to the faculty through PLCs (green).
A10. Administrative team will prioritize and mesh work into the ninety-day plan for the culture audit, safety audit, and ninety-day plan (green).	ERL/principal/administrative team	Prior to th interviews being conducted, interview questions will be provided to the faculty. The goal is for 100 percent of the faculty to be able to provide information as to their ability to integrate the school's mission and vision into their daily instruction. Results of the survey will be shared with faculty at bimonthly staff meeting (green).

If we are not successful, we will:
Reexamine the data within the school's leadership team to determine where the breakdown occurred and how to restructure the process to accommodate for it.
In 120 days, we will know we are successful when:
Seventy-five percent of teachers demonstrate mastery of instructional nonnegotiables evident through walkthrough data.
The measures/evidences we will use are:
Walkthrough data: 100 percent of teachers will have walkthroughs, with the expectation of no less than 75 percent of teachers demonstrating effective instructional nonnegotiables.

A11. Teachers will have individualized training, refine growth plans, and participate in professional growth activities based on areas of deficiency in demonstrating nonnegotiables. PGP work session scheduled for content area to document specific evidence of progress toward growth objective to promote accountability. Comparative sets of walkthrough data will be analyzed during an instructional work session to identify instruction next steps.	ER team, PLC leads, administrative team	As walkthroughs have been conducted, administrators will share the results of walkthroughs and how instructional nonnegotiables are met.
A12. A teacher survey will be conducted based on specific deficiencies identified in culture audit findings. Faculty meeting scheduled to plan action steps from survey.	Specific names	The administrative team will compile individual and group feedback and share (administrative team includes principal, ap, counselors, ER team).
A13. The district safety committee will reconvene to analyze the culture audit results and to assimilate the teacher survey results to create action steps/processes for addressing appropriate concerns.	Specific names	
A14. Administrative team members/district employees will participate in a work session to aggregate all discipline data and create a more efficient system for gathering the data. Three priority sections will be identified along with steps for implementation	Specific names	

If we are not successful, we will:
Provide additional support to individual teachers as determined by data.
Provide additional job-embedded professional development for deficient areas.
In 150 days, we will know we are successful when:
The measures/evidences we will use are:

150 Days Action Strategies	Who is on point?	How will we communicate it?
A15. Administrative team will work with stakeholder group representatives to merge all school plans into one manageable, governing plan with action steps.	Administrative team	All stakeholders will receive a plan of action reflecting all plans combined.
A16. Administrative team and PLC leaders will focus a portion of each meeting during this period on creating a systematic flow chart for teacher rewards/student rewards for success (that is, leadership roles, assemblies, conferences, choice).	Administrative team including PLC chairs	PLC leaders' meetings will have a predetermined agenda for this purpose.
A17. A consistent schedule of learning walks to include the ATC teachers and middle school reps as an initial effort at instructional alignment. These events will be prefaced with a preconference and followed by debriefing and creation of next steps.	Specific names here from administrative team	Schedule with agenda communicated with stakeholders and presented at board meeting.

If we are not successful, we will:

Examine the mission and vision survey results to ascertain specifically which stakeholder groups are the least able to clearly articulate the school's mission and vision and then restructure our media campaign approach to target selected stakeholder groups.

Examine processes for learning walks. Use plus/delta information from meetings to look for root cause of issues.

Appendix C

A Guide for Using Data Questions

Note: It is most effective to answer the questions as a leadership team.

1. Questions to answer: How are our processes working?
2. What does the data or information tell us?

- This question is asking for a general summary of the data or information through the eyes of those analyzing it.
- It is not a value judgment as to why the data or information are what they are.

For example: Regarding the data collected from the process for the Tier III Semester report in Eastern Kentucky in 2010.
What the data or information tells us is:

- 95 percent of reports were submitted by midnight on January 7, 2011
- 73 percent of the reports had three SMART goals based on the SIG
- 14 percent of the SMART goals included both horizon (over three years) and formative (quarterly or semester goals)
- 76 percent of the reports had complete data
- 73 percemt of the reports had complete data including data questions
- 99 percent of the reports indicate RTI processes in place
- 21 percent of the reports have interventions clearly outlined for explore and plan

3. What does the data or information not tell us?

*   This question is asking for any other data or factors that may impact this data or information not clearly indicated by the data.

For example: Regarding the data collected from the process for the Tier III Semester report.
What the data or information does not tell us is:

*   Who completed the report (district, school, principal, teams)
*   Who answered the data questions
*   If the people who completed the reports that did not answer the data questions attended coaching sessions
*   If the report data was weather related
*   Which teams attended voluntary coaching sessions/if that helped
*   How much time was required to complete the report
*   If this report is what is going on in the schools or if it is an add-on for compliance

4. What are the causes for celebration?

*   This question is primarily based on the data or processes that are in progress because the data indicated it should happen.

For example: Regarding the data collected from the process for the Tier III Semester report.
Causes for celebration are:

*   All but two reports are in
*   The majority appear to have a clear understanding of SMART goals
*   The majority addressed RTI with clear understanding
*   The majority addressed the SIG SMART goals

5. What are the opportunities for improvement?

*   This question's answer should be based on the data or processes that are in progress because the data indicated it should happen.

For example: Regarding the data collected from the process for the Tier III Semester report.
Opportunities for improvement are:

- There is a need for understanding of how the SIG SMART goals need to include quarterly, semester, or test administration predictive goals as well as end of the year goals. The in-process goals are to help guide staff as they move forward on a regular basis as opposed to at the end of the year. Many have the data after the fact, once the test is given, but have not projected what scores should be expected along the way.
- There is a need for understanding how to answer the data questions
- Ensure/verify that the principals are the lead in deployment of the SIG
- Determine if there is a better method for establishing the due date (earlier/later)
- Ensure that everyone knows the data available on OPEN HOUSE
- From the content: because it is a new requirement, clear understanding of senior interventions, explore and plan interventions, and what is available
- From the content: many new programs and processes being started that we cannot determine effectiveness from things evident in the reports. Not clear whether fidelity measures are being built into training and PD.

6. **What are the next steps?**

- This question wants to know what activities are going to occur to address the opportunities for improvement

For example: Regarding the data collected from the process for the Tier III Semester report.
Next steps:

- Share the data and information as well as the comments about the reports with the principals involved
- Share the reports with the partners who will be attending the review sessions
- Verify all logistics with participants for review meetings
- Ensure that all know the agenda and questions they will be asked
- Conduct review meetings
- Determine information that needs to go to schools at the end of the meetings and share
- Conduct survey of participants for process improvement
- Work with partners and schools as needed across the second semester

Additional work samples may be found in appendices D through G, accessed online at https://rowman.com/ISBN/9781475843064/Without-Trumpets-Continuous-Educational-Improvement-Journey-to-Sustainability.

CONTENTS

Glossary

Acronym	What the Letters Mean	What It Is
ASSIST	Adaptive System of School Improvement Support Tools	AdvancED technology system used for school improvement planning
BOE	Board of Education	Governance system at state and local levels
CAO	Chief Academic Officer	Local education position
CCSSO	Council of Chief State School Officers	Organization of state officers
CT4GC	Coteaching for Gap Closure	Kentucky Department of Education approach to coteaching for teachers of students with disabilities and regular education
DE	Distinguished Educators	Highly skilled education specialists; earliest iteration in Kentucky
DPP	Director of Pupil Personnel	Local position required by Kentucky statute
EMO	External Management Organization (Operator)	One of the choices for governance in priority schools through school improvement grants
ER	Education Recovery	All the processes used to address needs in priority schools in Kentucky; District 180

Acronym	What the Letters Mean	What It Is
ERD	Education Recovery Director	Three coordinator supervisory positions in District 180 located in the three regions of Kentucky
ERL	Education Recovery Leader	One designated for each priority school to work with school principal and supervise ER team
ERS	Education Recovery Specialists	Two designated math and language arts specialists assigned to each priority school; full time
ESSA	Every Student Succeeds Act	Legislation passed by U.S. Congress in 2016; current iteration of 1965 Elementary and Secondary Education Act; replaces NCLB
HB176	House Bill 176	Kentucky legislation establishing District 180
HSE	Highly Skilled Educators	Highly skilled specialists; second iteration; forerunner of ER
KDE	Kentucky Department of Education	Kentucky governance structure in the Workforce and Education Cabinet with responsibility for public education in Kentucky
KERA	Kentucky Education Reform Act	Legislation passed in Kentucky in 1990
KOSSA	Kentucky Occupational Skills Standards Assessment	Kentucky exam to assist high schools and community/ technical schools in determining entrance
LA	Language Arts	
MAP	Measure of Academic Progress	One of the formative assessments used by some schools
NCLB	No Child Left Behind	Legislation passed by U.S. Congress in 2001; next iteration of 1965 Elementary and Secondary Education Act
NGA	National Governors Association	Original authorizer of a set of common core standards
PD	Professional Development	Name given to strategies used to build teacher/administrator capacity through workshops, etc.
PDSA	Plan-Do-Study-Act (also PDCheckA or Plan Inquire Act)	Continuous improvement cycle

Acronym	What the Letters Mean	What It Is
PLA	Persistently Low Achieving	Federal name given to schools that meet certain criteria. Used interchangeably in this book with priority schools.
PLC	Professional Learning Community	Structure for collaboration based on some common problem or work-alike grouping
RTI	Response to Intervention	Federally directed program to address the needs of students with disabilities; expanded in many places to provide interventions for any level of performance in progressive schools. May be renamed in any location.
RtT	Race to the Top	Competitive grant program through the U.S. Department of Education
SACS	Southern Association of Colleges and Schools; now AdvancED	National accrediting agency
SB1	Senate Bill 1 (2009, 2017)	Kentucky legislation post-KERA addressing school issues
SBDM	School Based Decision-Making Council	Kentucky legislated local group in each school providing guidance for teacher hiring, curriculum choice, and day-to-day operations of the school
SIG	School Improvement Grant	Federal funds available during the Obama administration to states providing support for school improvement. Funds primarily used in Kentucky for District 180.
SPED	Special Education	Kentucky name for services for students with disabilities
30-60-90	30-60-90-Day Planning Process	Brainchild of Dr. Joseph Murphy; organizational and management tools vital to improvement planning in Kentucky education
USDOE	U.S. Department of Education	Federal cabinet position and structure responsible for regulations, deployment, and monitoring of congressional authorized legislation

Bibliography

Beshear, Steve, and Dan Hassert. 2017. *People Over Politics: A Stronger Kentucky.* Kentucky: A Stronger Kentucky, Inc.

Bonilla, S., and T. Dee. 2017. *The Effects of School Reform Under NCLB Waivers: Evidence from Focus Schools in Kentucky.* CEPA Working Paper No.17-05. Stanford Center for Educational Policy Analysis. http://cepa.stanford.edu/wp17-05.

City-Data. 2017. "Jefferson County–KY." Accessed October 17. http://www.city-data.com/county/Jefferson_County-KY.html.

CREDO (Center for Research on Education Outcomes) at Stanford University. 2017. "CREDO at Stanford University Releases National Study on School Closure." August 24. http://credo.stanford.edu/pdfs/Closure%20Press%20Release.pdf.

Dragoset, L., J. Thomas, M. Nermann, J. Deke, S. James-Burdimy, C. K. Graczewski, A. Boyle, Rachel Upton, C. Tanenbaum, and J. Griffin. *School Improvement Grants Implementation nd Effectiveness.* Washington, DC: U.S. Department of Education, Institute of Education Sciences, National Center for Education Evaluation and Regional Assistance. https://www.mathematica-mpr.com/our-publications-and-findings/publications/sig-implementation-and-effectiveness.

Evan, A., M. Huberman, B. Means, K. Mitchell, L. Shear, J. Shkolnik, S. Becky, et al. 2016, August. "Evaluation of the Bill and Melinda Gates Foundation's High School Grants Initiative: 2001–2005 Final Report." The National Evaluation of High School Transformation, American Institutes for Research and SRI International. https://docs.gatesfoundation.org/documents/Year4EvaluationAIRSRI.pdf.

Gleason, P., M. Clark, C. C. Tuttle, and E. Dwoyer. 2010. *The Evaluation of Charter School Impacts: Final Report* (NCEE 2010-4029). Washington, DC: National Center for Education Evaluation and Regional Assistance, Institute of Education Sciences, U.S. Department of Education.

Kentucky Department of Education. 2010. *Kentucky Department of Education District Grant Application for School Improvement Funds—Leslie County.* June

1. https://education.ky.gov/federal/progs/sigi/Documents/10-07-22%20Priority-Leslie%20Co%20HS.pdf.

Kentucky Department of Education. 2015. *Kentucky Department of Education District Grant Application for School Improvement Funds—Jefferson County.* September. https://education.ky.gov/federal/progs/sigi/Documents/15-09-10%20 Priority-Valley%20HS.pdf.

Kentucky Department of Education. 2017. *Kentucky's Learning Goals and Academic Expectations.* Accessed October 16. https://education.ky.gov/curriculum/ standards/kyacadstand/Documents/Kentuckys%20Learning%20Goals%20and%20 Academic%20Expectations.pdf.

Kentucky Department of Education. 2010. *Jefferson County Public Schools 2009–2010 Report Card.* Accessed October 17, 2017. https://applications.education. ky.gov/schoolreportcardarchive/default.aspx.

Larson, Jim. 2015. "In Kentucky, a Collaborative Approach to School Turn-around." The New Teacher Project. December 8. https://tntp.org/blog/post/ in-kentucky-a-collaborative-approach-to-school-turnaround.

Lusi, Dr. Susan F., and John Schneider. 2017. "State Development Network for High School Turnaround—Kentucky State Diagnostic Report." *Mass Insight.* Presented February 9 to Kentucky School Board. file:///C:/Users/Susan/AppData/Local/ Packages/Microsoft.MicrosoftEdge_8wekyb3d8bbwe/TempState/Downloads/ XIII_ImprovementWorkPPT_0.pdf.

Private School Review. 2003–2017. *Jefferson County.* https://www.privateschool review.com/kentucky/jefferson-county.

Sparks, Sarah D. 2017. "Report Roundup: School Improvement." *Education Weekly.* January 24. http://www.edweek.org/ew/articles/2017/01/25/school-improvement. html.

"TELL Kentucky: District 180 Longitudinal Analysis." New Teacher Center. www. newteachercenter.org.

Trump, Donald. 2017. "Remarks of President Trump at Signing of Executive Order on Federalism Education." April 26. https://www.whitehouse.gov/the-press-office/2017/04/26/remarks-president-trump-signing-executive-order-federalism-education.

U.S. Department of Education. 2014. "Effective and Sustainable Turnaround in Rural Kentucky." April 29. https://sites.ed.gov/progress/2014/04/ effective-and-sustainable-turnaround-in-rural-kentucky/.

U.S. Department of Education. 2017. "School Improvement Grants—Program Description." Accessed October 16. https://www2.ed.gov/programs/sif/index.html.

Vance, J. D. *Hillbilly Elegy.* London, KY: Harper Collins, 2016.

Index

Index

About the Authors

Kelly A. Foster is a Kentucky native whose family has lived in Kentucky for generations. She attended public schools including public universities where she earned her BA and MA from Eastern Kentucky University and MA in administration and EdD from Morehead State University.

After teaching English in Madison and Montgomery County (Kentucky) Schools, Foster became principal in the Nicholas County Schools. She served as director of instruction in Montgomery County Schools for four years before joining the Kentucky Department of Education in 2009 as a highly skilled educator, then education recovery leader, and in 2013 became associate commissioner, the position she currently holds. Her favorite pastime is attending and talking about anything surrounding the University of Kentucky sports teams, especially football and basketball, and spending time at any beach, anywhere, anytime.

Susan G. Allred attended public schools in Albemarle and Gastonia, North Carolina, followed by receiving an AA from Gaston Community College, BA from UNC-Charlotte, MA from Gardner-Webb University, and an EdS from Appalachian State University, all in North Carolina. She taught social studies and English for twenty years at the middle and high school levels in Gaston County (North Carolina) followed by administrative school positions in Fort Mill (South Carolina), Transylvania (North Carolina), and Iredell-Statesville (North Carolina) school systems for nineteen years. In 2010 she joined the Kentucky Department of Education as an education recovery director for Eastern Kentucky followed by two interim associate commissioner roles at the Department of Education. Currently she mentors and consults with schools, districts, states, and organizations in a semi-retired manner from her home in Western North Carolina. She enjoys seeing her former students and mentees succeed and achieve and loves rocking on the porch.

Praise for *Without Trumpets*

"From 2007 to 2015, Kentucky's education system significantly improved its national reputation for innovation and reform. We strengthened support for the lowest performing schools through District 180 and the Educational Recovery Initiative focusing on increasing the capacity of teachers and administrators in those identified schools and giving all students a chance at a quality education."

—The Honorable Steve Beshear, Governor of Kentucky, 2007–2015

"An incredible book that will inform the practice for all of us working to improve the lives of children! I want to thank Kelly Foster and Susan Allred for their contribution to the field of education. This book delves into the lessons learned around a wide range of specific topics related to school improvement. Despite all that has been learned across the nation school improvement continues to encounter many barriers that have prevented lasting and sustainable reform. Whether it's external factors such as school-community relations, the political climate, or internal factors such as teacher and principal turnover or principal and teacher capacity—at any given low-performing school a myriad of challenges continue to exist. This book is an asset to the field of education as it provides real lessons learned from across many attempts at school improvement reform. In this book, education leaders can find a great deal of guidance specific to addressing existing barriers to sustainable and systemic school improvement."

—Carlas McCauley, director, Center on School Turnaround at WestEd

"With the implementation of Every Student Succeeds Act (ESSA) state education agency leaders must model intentional leadership for local districts about effectiveness and efficiency in reaching college and career goals with all students. States can learn much from each other about how to build sustainable processes to meet those goals. Kentucky's District 180 story is one such process to be shared."

—Chris Minnich, executive director, Council of Chief State School Officers, 2012–2018

"This book is as much for education leaders as it is for the communities that surround our schools and want to make a difference for our young people. Kelly and Susan give us reason for hope that educational excellence can be achieved anywhere if we are willing to come together, within and outside of the school house, in a spirit of shared responsibility and courageous honesty, celebrating even the smallest successes and recommitting daily to a march of continuous improvement together."

—Brigitte Blom Ramsey, executive director, Prichard Committee for Academic Excellence, Lexington, Kentucky